THE COUNTRY LIFE LIBRARY OF ANTIQUES

HORSE BRASSES

Horse Brasses

Peter C. D. Brears

COUNTRY LIFE BOOKS

N.B. All brasses, unless otherwise
stated, may be seen in the Kirk collection of the
Castle Museum, York.

Frontispiece
Detail from a painting of the Rush-bearing
Ceremony at Lymm, Cheshire in the 1840s; note the
trophies, brasses and bells on the fringed collar.

Published by Country Life Books
and distributed for them by
The Hamlyn Publishing Group Limited
London · New York · Sydney · Toronto
Astronaut House, Feltham, Middlesex, England

First published 1981
ISBN 0 600 32131 2

Set in 10pt Monophoto Garamond by
Tradespools Limited, Frome

Printed in England by
Hazell, Watson & Viney Limited,
Aylesbury

Contents

Introduction

OF ALL items connected with the English countryside none is more evocative of our rich rural past than the horse brass, conjuring up images of hot summer days in the harvest field, or of heavy-laden drays calling at the local pub. Some of the designs, cast in brightly polished metal, were apparently capable of turning away the 'evil eye', being used for this purpose since time immemorial. This is how most people still see the horse brass, but the truth presents a rather different picture.

Just 200 years ago, towards the end of the 18th century, the horse brass was virtually unknown. The horses might bear small brass plates pinned on to their harness, or have long worsted fringing around their collars. They might even be copiously decorated with trophies and garlands of ribbon on May Day, but they did not wear any of the ornamental hanging brasses so popular today. These were a product of the mid 19th-century flowering of English folk art, when the newly developed skills of the industrial craftsmen were diverted into a whole range of decorative items. This was the period of the Staffordshire pottery figure, the cast iron chimney ornament and the glass frigger. None of their designs was based on the precepts of fashionable academic taste, but instead each was drawn from the craftsman's own experience adapted to the particular needs of those whom he served. As the pattern-makers who made the earliest cast brasses had previously worked on armorial crests for the aristocracy, it is not surprising to find a strong heraldic influence in their designs, although they were quick to add contemporary figures of carters and ploughmen, of farmyard animals or of modern railway locomotives as required.

As a result of their skill and ingenuity, there are now some 2,000 different brasses in existence, each with a characteristic range of decorative features. It is not surprising that they now form an interesting field for the collector, for, in addition to the inherent beauty of their design and materials, it is still possible for a person of modest means to acquire an interesting and rewarding collection. In the following pages the history, manufacture and identification of horse brasses are considered in detail in the hope that this will lead to an increased appreciation of their finer qualities.

Peter C. D. Brears

1. Medieval horse decorations from Ixworth, Suffolk. Ashmolean Museum, Oxford.

CHAPTER ONE

Development of Horse Brasses

THERE CAN be few sights so pleasing to the eye as a well-groomed heavy horse, its coat brushed to a high gloss, its mane and tail carefully plaited with bright ribbons, and its harness resplendent with a rich array of shining brasses. Every detail reflects the waggoner's pride in his team, and represents many hours of patient preparation. Today the heavy horse is seldom seen in his full splendour, except at agricultural shows or in those towns where brewery drays still make their regular deliveries, but his decorations continue to feature in many domestic interiors. Enter any country pub or cottage, and there behind the bar, along the beams and around the fireplace there is likely to appear a fine display of horse brasses. Each one will have its own distinctive shape and design, perhaps including an abstract pattern, or a detailed miniature representation of some popular subject. It is quite possible that many of these have never come into contact with a horse, however, for their chief purpose now is to serve as attractive ornaments wherever a cosy rural atmosphere is required. Although they do have the unfailing ability to evoke a feeling of nostalgia for those bygone days when the pace of life could still be measured by the steady plodding of the draught horse, it was not for this purpose that they were first intended. Indeed it is necessary to go back into prehistory in order to trace their origins.

Probably the earliest decorations to have been found in this country were those discovered by H. R. Hughes of Kinmel Park, Denbighshire, on 26 March 1868 (Franks, Sir Wollaston, *Archaeologia* 43, 1868, p. 556. For details of further prehistoric horse furniture see *Frozen Tombs; The Culture and Art of the Ancient Tribes of Siberia*, British Museum Publications, 1978). They were excavated from the foot of a crag forming part of a hill known as 'Parc-y-meirch' or the Park of Horses, a former defensive site. Dating from the late bronze age (*c.* 750 to 400 B.C.) the entire hoard comprised some 90 pieces of cast bronze horse furniture, many being purely practical in the form of buckles, slides, and terrets. There were also sets of decorative 'brasses', however, consisting of three pairs of irregular oval bronze plates with hanging loops, through which passed a bar of the same metal. Each plate averaged $2\frac{3}{4}$ inches across, and most had a slight pimple in the centre, resembling the boss of a round shield. The loops showed signs of wear, and in some cases were almost worn through. It is interesting to note that one 'brass' which hangs in front of the massive loop of another has a piece about the size of a thumb nail entirely worn away with constant rubbing. Clusters of round 'brasses' of this kind must have produced a lively jingling sound with every movement of the horse, drawing attention to the importance of the rider as he approached, while also enhancing his appearance. These early specimens are now divided between the collections of the National Museum of Wales in Cardiff, and the Hull City Museums.

From the Roman period there is very little evidence for the use of horse brasses in this country, although it has been suggested that a number of bronze disc ornaments found in Roman graves were used in this way. A series illustrated in R. A. Brown's *Horse Brasses* measure from 1 inch to 1¾ inches in diameter, and are decorated with concentric borders, fluted rims and inscribed ring-and-dot designs. Each example is linked by a broad hanger to a plain bronze ring around which the end of a strap or belt might be sewn, but whether for use by man or by horse is still uncertain.

Horse decorations reappeared in quite a sophisticated form in the high medieval period, when small metal pendants were attached to the harness. They made a characteristic ringing sound as the horse progressed; in the prologue of *Canterbury Tales* Chaucer described how the trappings of the monk's horse were so arranged that:

> whan he rood, men myght his brydel heere
> Gynglen in a whystlynge wynd als cleere
> And eek as loud as dooth the chapel belle.

One group of these small brasses was presented to the Ashmolean Museum in 1927, having originated at Ixworth in Suffolk. Their designs bore some resemblance to those of modern brasses, the first being a flat round flower of eight petals, the second, a broad-armed cross, and the third a flat disc with a hemispherical domed boss at its centre, each one having a small round hanger rising from its top edge. These brasses were exceptionally plain, however, most medieval examples being cast in bronze and richly decorated with armorial devices in coloured enamel. Lions, peacocks and coronets are among the motifs which have been recorded, but of far greater interest are those whose armorials enable their exact dates to be firmly established. Two fine examples in the Salisbury and South Wiltshire Museum illustrate this point quite clearly. One found at Clarendon Palace shows the arms of Sir Robert Fitzpaine, Governor of Corfe Castle in 1304, while the other, found on Mere Down, has the arms of St Maur on one side and Lovell on the other, Nicholas St Maur and Muriel Lovell having been married in 1351.

There is little evidence to suggest how harness was decorated in the late-medieval or early post-medieval periods, but the few surviving cast bronze pieces show that the founder was still capable of producing good quality work. The harness bosses of the 16th century were apparently being cast in sand in a similar manner to modern brasses, and might have their domes enriched with openwork ribs or fleur-de-lis designs within neatly scrolled borders (e.g., Ashmolean Museum, Oxford, 1927–6477, unprovenanced, and 1913–815, from George Street, Oxford).

During the 18th century it became increasingly fashionable for the nobility and gentry to display their family crests on their state and semi-state vehicles. On the carriages, the full coat of arms was usually painted on the door panels, while on the harness finely chased silver or silver-plated crests were attached to the face piece which hung from the brow-band, the blinkers, the saddle, the side straps, and perhaps the martingale, a strap which passed down the breast of the horse from the bottom of the collar to the girth. Full state harness decorated in this manner was truly magnificent, especially when made in the unique royal blue leather reserved for the use of the sovereign. By the mid 19th century most members of the upper and middle classes had adopted the wearing of some form of fine white-metal harness decoration, elaborate monograms being extremely popular for those who were unable to boast true armorials of their own.

It will have been noticed that all the harness decorations referred to above were worn by the horses of knightly or aristocratic families, no mention being made of the heavy-horse harness used for common draught or agricultural work. Contrary to popular belief, the horse brass as it is known today is a relatively modern innovation, and not the product of centuries of development. It is extremely difficult to find any brass dating from before the mid 19th century, and similarly difficult to trace any information on brasses in early literature or illustrations. Volumes such as Thomas Tusser's *Five Hundred Good Points of Husbandry* of 1573 and Gervase Markham's *Maister-Peece* of 1636 make no reference to horse brasses, while Pyne's comprehensive *Microcosm* published in 1806 only shows small brass escutcheons on the blinkers and saddles of a few horses. Even as late as 1855, J. S. Morton's *Encyclopedia of Agriculture* made no mention of brasses in its chapter on harness, and only illustrated a single round plate on the blinker of one horse.

The earlier methods of decorating working harness relied entirely on the skills of the saddler, as clearly shown in a full-faced bridle of 1744 now preserved in the Museum of Leathercraft at Walsall. Here the decoration is worked in leather thongs 'sewn' through the bridle almost like embroidery, a simple, economical, but still effective, technique. The leather might also have its surface enriched with tooled decoration, Terry Keegan noting a housen having the date '1769' raced in together with the initials 'T.H.' and a floral design which occurs both in the corners and around the edges of the piece (Keegan, T. *The Heavy Horse, Its Harness and Decoration*, London, 1973, p. 125). Stitching could provide a similar medium for decoration too, being used to mark fancy geometric or naturalistic patterns on the bridle, the saddle, and on the broad ends of the straps.

Richer and more colourful effects were obtained by the addition of thick woollen fringes which were either sewn around the housen or, in the southern counties, nailed beneath the protective leather hoods of the long belfries mounted over the horses' necks. To some, all these forms of harness decoration were both unsightly and unnecessary, Henry Stevens censuring their use in his *Book of the Farm* of 1855:

With regard to ornamenting farm harness, it never appears, in my estimation, to greater advantage, than when quite plain, and of the best materials and workmanship. Brass or plated buckles and browbands, worsted rosettes, and broad bands of leather tattooed with filigree sewing, serve only to load and cover the horses when at work, to create trouble, collect dirt, and at best display a wasteful and vulgar taste in the owner. Whatever temptation there might be in towns to show off the grandeur of the teams of rival establishments, such displays of vanity are incompatible with the country.

In spite of this purely practical approach, most men wished to reflect their pride in their animals by grooming and decorating them to the greatest advantage. This was particularly noticeable on such important occasions as feast days, the hirings, market days, or when going to a ploughing match or agricultural show. Here every team would be subject to close examination, and the quality of both farmer and waggoner judged accordingly.

Until recently, the most celebrated event in the rural year was May Day, for it marked the passing of winter, and the start of the warm summer months. It was the time of germination, of growth, and of fertility, when lads and lasses went into the woods in the early morning to gather May blossom, and to bring back the maypole ready for the afternoon's dancing. Up to the late 18th or early 19th centuries, the ox was still the most important draught animal on the land and so great ox teams were assembled to drag the pole back to the village.

They have twentie or fortie yoke [pairs] of oxen, every oxe havyng a sweete nose-gaie of flowers tyed on the tippe of his hornes, and these oxen drawe home this Maie poole, which is covered all over with flowers and herbes,

wrote Stubbes (Hone, W. *The Every-Day Book*, 1827, Vol. 1, p. 547), while Strutt described how the maypole was 'drawn by eight fine oxen decorated with scarfs, ribbons, and flowers of divers colours; and the tips of their horns were embellished with gold' (*Ibid*, p. 553). As the horse replaced the ox on the land, so it took the ox's place in ceremonials of this type, inheriting the traditional decorations.

In fact, the custom of decorating horses on May Day eventually became the sole survivor of the old festivities, continuing long after the gathering of the May blossom, the May games, and the maypole had all disappeared. In North Yorkshire in 1899 it was still usual for the stable boys and draymen to garnish their horses' heads with ribbons begged from the shops to mark 'horse ribbon day'. In the bigger towns where large numbers of horse-drawn vehicles were in daily use, the May-Day celebrations grew to become an important institution for the equestrian community, with thousands of decorated horses appearing in the streets. As in the country as a whole, the London carters traditionally paraded on May Day, but in 1886 they transferred to Whit Monday for the first time. This change was due to the activities of the London Cart Horse Parade Society founded in the previous year, its purpose being to improve the general condition and treatment of cart horses in the metropolis.

Although the horse had adopted the ox's ribbons and flowers for special occasions, it had not adopted any metallic harness decorations, for these had never been worn. Towards the end of the 18th century, however, small brass plates began to appear on heavy-horse harness. Usually they were restricted to rounds, ovals, or squares fixed on to the blinkers and the corners of the saddles. It was in these precise locations that the aristocratic coach-horse was already wearing its owner's heraldic crest, and it would appear that these early brasses were simply made to enable the waggoner to show off his horses by imitating his social superiors.

Probably the earliest English horse brass is now in the Salisbury and South Wiltshire Museum. It is a small heart-shaped plate engraved with the date '1776'. A further heart-shaped brass in Birmingham Museum is dated 1830, but this is rather suspect, since the numbers have been punched into the brass, probably on some later occasion. The same collection contains a circular brass bearing the inscription 'MAUNDERS ROYAL MENAGERIE 1839' around a small central lion. Although Maunder's Menagerie existed in 1839, being mentioned in Charles Dickens's *Old Curiosity Shop*, the accomplished design and quality of this specimen suggest that it actually dates from the late 19th century at the earliest. In brief, horse brasses dating from before the 1850s are of the greatest rarity, and their claims of authenticity should be thoroughly examined before making a purchase.

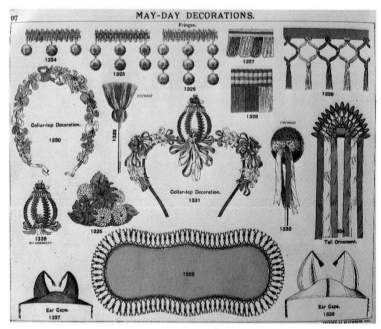

2. May-day decorations from Thacker's catalogue of 1895.

3. 'Thomas Powell, 1778' – one of the earliest horse brasses.

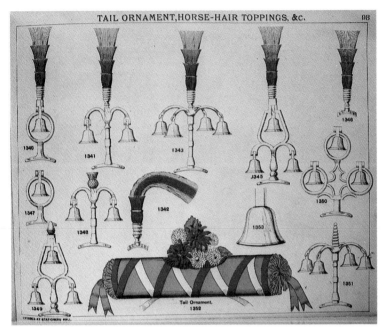

4. Tail ornaments and horse-hair toppings from Thacker's catalogue of 1895.

One of the most fascinating records in the development of the horse brass is a painting of *c.* 1850 in the Castle Museum at York. It depicts the rush-bearing ceremony at Lymm in Cheshire, the cart loaded with its square-cut pillar of rushes being preceded by a side of Morris dancers as it processes to the church, the band following on behind. The horses drawing the cart are decorated in their full finery, and show the transition between the old woollen fringing and the developing brasses. The collar of each horse is covered in a deep pink fringe over which are hung rows of rumbler and open-mouthed latten bells, while from their heads rise high trophies containing the 'v.R.' monogram of Queen Victoria, and red, white and blue flags. These appear to have been worked in ribbon, greenery and wire bound with coloured woollen yarn in a similar manner to the modern Scottish decorations. As for brasses, these are restricted to small octagons on the blinkers, back bands, housens and hame straps, except for a single hanging face piece on each horse in the form of a round sunburst.

The mid 19th century marked a period of change in British agriculture, a period of increasing confidence and success following the depressed years after the Napoleonic wars. As H. Robinson Carter commented (Carter, H. R. 'The Age of Horse Brasses', *The Connoisseur*, Vol.

5. Stags from Fairbairn's *Book of Crests*.

LXXXVII, 1931, p. 214), it was during the 1850s that Surtees' Major Yammerton dismissed his Agent, Mr Bullrush, and took advantage of

... the practical, easy working Drainage Act! and consequently began to thrive. As well as acquiring Squire Trefoil's famous Cockaded Coach, he also bought new implements and some stout horses, and when he and old Solomon were doing a little business at the markets or fairs about 1860 he was probably invited, and probably refused, to buy a set of the new fangled Brass Horse Ornaments that were just being made by an enterprising firm who wanted to get some of the farmer's profits.

It is interesting to discover that no brasses were produced to mark the Great Exhibition of 1851, the Crimean War of 1853–6, or those nationally important figures Prince Albert (d. 1861) and Lord Palmerston (d. 1865). A few years later, however, most popular and patriotic subjects were being commemorated by the horse-brass founders. These included Lord Randolph Churchill in the 1880s, Disraeli, the Earl of Beaconsfield (d. 1881), his opponent, Gladstone, the Jubilees of 1887

6. (*Top*) Stag brasses based on heraldic designs. (*Bottom*) Heraldic brasses.

and 1897, and the Boer War (1899–1901). From the above evidence, it is suggested that the modern horse brass, mass-produced in sand-moulds (albeit by hand techniques) for sale throughout the country, was essentially a product of the 1860s and early 1870s, having gradually developed from the initial influence of the carriage horses' heraldic crests.

The earliest of these brasses are most likely to have been relatively simple, their shapes including the heart, crescent, star and sunflash. These are the most common forms for those rare handmade brasses probably the work of gypsies or itinerant tinkers during the late 18th or early 19th centuries. From these basic shapes, the founders were able to develop more complex designs drawn from a variety of sources. As the waggoners wanted their horses to be as well decorated as those of the aristocracy, they found pseudo-heraldic brasses especially attractive. Lions, stags, unicorns, eagles and other heraldic beasts were all popular, particularly in those areas where they bore resemblance to the armorials of the leading county family. Similar pride could be shown by wearing brasses featuring symbols of local significance, such as the mitre rising

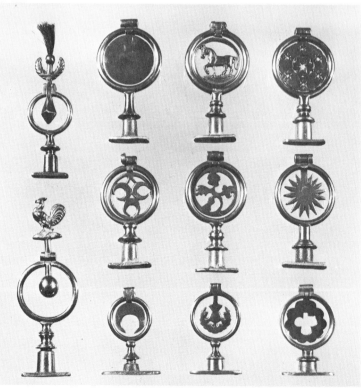

from a coronet of the Prince-Bishops of Durham, the Bear and Ragged Staff of the Earls of Warwick, or the Staffordshire Knot; the latter two were of great interest in Walsall, the centre of the harness trade, and together form the badge of the town. It was here that the silver crests for carriage harness were made by those highly skilled craftsmen, the heraldic chasers. They already possessed a deep knowledge of all the pattern-making techniques on which the developing trade in horse brasses depended, in addition to having access to a wealth of design sources, including volumes such as Fairbairn's *Book of Crests*. This single work contained hundreds of highly finished engraved illustrations of true heraldic crests, and provided a wide range of potential designs for brasses.

On a national level, horse brasses were cast with patriotic symbols,

7. (*Opposite, top*) Plough horses at the Great All England Ploughing Match, Asthall Farm, Burford, 1976.   8. (*Opposite, bottom*) Fly (head) terrets.
9. (*Below*) Terret bells.

including the rose, the thistle, the shamrock, and the harp. These were either used individually, or with the rose, thistle and shamrock combined to form the 'Bonny Bunch of Roses' – the symbol of a united Britain widely used from the years of the Napoleonic Wars. Further designs were firmly based within the popular folk tradition, including hunting and sporting themes, while others, intended to appeal directly to the carter, showed a whole range of farmyard subjects.

Although horses were occasionally weighed down beneath a vast load of harness decoration for competitions or shows, the normal English cart harness was usually decorated in quite a restrained manner. Probably the oldest form of brass harness decoration to have continued in use up to the present day is the rosette or boss mounted over the junction of the browband, cheek strap, throat lash or head strap. These are usually either conical or dome-shaped, and appear just below the ear on both sides of the head. Then came the face piece, a brass mounted on a broad strap of leather and either buckled around or sewn on to the browband so that it hung down the centre of the forehead. A small brass escutcheon on the centre of the blinker and probably a brass plate hinged over the nose-band completed the decoration of the bridle, except for the fly (or head) terret. This was a vertical brass ornament which screwed on to a boss mounted on top of the head piece. Usually it took the form of a circular band of brass within which swung either a plain disc or a miniature version of a face-piece design, the light flashing from its reflective surface. These 'swingers' might be counterbalanced by a solid sphere of brass causing them to rotate completely as the horse nodded his head. Other forms of terret branched sideways to support miniature swinging discs or open-mouthed bells, while others terminated in tall plumes of red, white, or blue hair, their rigidity being increased by decorative binding bands of brass.

Decoration on the collar could include a coloured woollen fringing sewn around the back edge, but this has not been popular since before the First World War. Much more common was decoration on the hame plate, a long brass plate mounted on the strap which linked the curving tips of the hames. One favourite design showed three passant horses standing on a plain rectangular plate, but others were made with rounded ends and a circular area at the centre on which appeared a wide variety of designs to match those of the accompanying face pieces and fly terrets. A number of small brasses might also be found on the housen. Originally this panel of leather projecting backwards from the top of the collar had been large enough to keep the rain off the horse's withers in wet weather, being stood up vertically whenever it was fine. Now it is somewhat reduced in size, becoming a small semicircular addition to the collar, more ornamental than purposeful.

10. Hame plates.

From the bottom of the collar a broad leather strap extended down between the front legs, to buckle on to the girth. This breast plate, or martingale, prevented the collar from riding up or the girth from slipping backwards, but also appears to have been used for carrying a number of brasses. Usually two, three or four brasses were mounted one above the other down the horse's breast, the carter often buying them ready made in this form from the saddler. Breast plates could grow to an enormous size, however, one collected by H. Robinson Carter having eleven face pieces mounted in two rows separated by five small oval or rectangular brass escutcheons (Carter, H. R. 'English Horse Amulets', *The Connoisseur*, Vol. LXV, 1916, p. 150).

Passing down the horse, the decoration of the cart saddle was usually

11. Clydesdales at a ploughing match, their high square housens decorated with bright worsted fringing.

quite simple, a small brass being fixed on each corner of the leather housing, a threaded boss mounted over the wooden frame of the saddle, occasionally being provided for bells and plumes matching those of the fly terret.

A similar boss might also be fixed on the crupper, while further decorative side straps showing two, three or more face pieces could be hung down the loins and hips of the horse. Thus equipped, complete with decorated reins and rein hangers, the heavy horse looked his best, his glossy coat providing an ideal foil for the robustly elegant combination of dark polished leather and shining brass. It is not surprising that both artists and writers were impressed by his appearance. Writing in 1904, Gertrude Jekyll provides an excellent account (Jekyll, G. *Old West Surrey*, London, 1904, p. 211) of the place of horse decorations in the old West Surrey countryside she knew so well.

There was an amicable rivalry among the carters as to the dressing of their horses, for the brightly polished brass ornaments and the gay rosettes of worsted ribbon were the carters' own property, and when not on the horses were often arranged as a trophy over the cottage fireplace. Foremost amongst these ornaments were the ear-bells with their upright plume of black and white, or red and yellow horse-hair . . . Sometimes in place of the plume there was the ornament of three tinkling bells, or the circular brass plate, hinged at the top, that flashed as it swung, often turning right over as Dobbin tossed his head, and there was a brass plate with shaped edge, engraved with a horse and cart or some other device that went on the nose-band. Then there were the 'face-pieces' in a great variety of pattern; also used below the collar, three or four one above another. The love of decorating his horses is still a matter of pleasant pride to the good carter, and when I see a well-looking team, made unusually smart for the road or town, I know that the carter is a good fellow, who takes a right pride in his work and cattle.

Writing about the same time, Bernard Weaver was already noting a decline in the quality of horse decoration (Weaver, B. 'Horse Amulets',

12. A pair of horses decorated for a ploughing match. Beautifully groomed, with brasses gleaming, they await their turn in the competition, while sharing their hay.

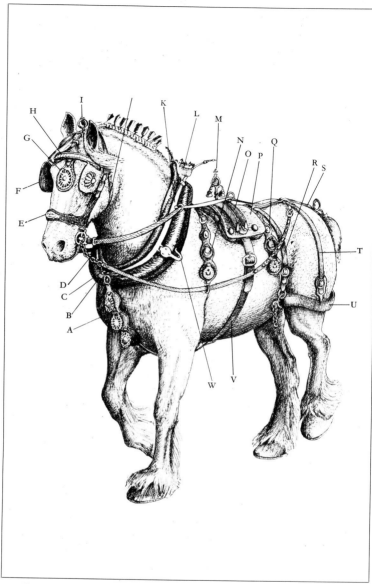

13. Harness for a heavy horse: A breast plate (martingale), B collar, C leading rein, D driving rein, E nose-band, F blinker, G face piece, H browband, I fly terret, J throat lash (head strap), K hame, L hame plate, M harness bells, N rein hanger, O channel, P high-bridged pad, Q side strap, R loin strap, S crupper, T carrying strap, U breeching, V girth, W hame tug.

14. Plough horses at Asthall Farm, Burford, 1976.

The Country Home, September 1908, p. 268). Mr Weaver posed several questions:

What is the advantage of loading a draught-horse with as many as eighteen brasses—a weight of over 6 lbs? Is it kindness to the horse? Many carters and more farmers, however, still look upon their brasses with a lingering affection and continue using them for the sake of appearance.

Although we shall never see the return of the traditional horse-powered economy mourned by Mr Weaver, it is pleasing to know that the heavy horse and his decorations have not only withstood the pressures of the last 80 years, but are now enjoying a new and developing popularity. Long may this continue.

CHAPTER TWO

Manufacturing

It is very difficult to obtain any reliable information regarding the early makers of horse brasses, even for the 18th and early 19th centuries when documentation is relatively plentiful. The accounts of both brass-founders and sheet metal workers still survive, as do the advertisements and notices they placed in local newspapers, but nowhere do they mention decorative horse brasses. This would indicate that the makers of this period were not well-established craftsmen, but were more likely to be either itinerant tinkers or small-time metalworkers carrying out a variety of services within their particular area. Men of this type were relatively common up to the end of the last century, travelling through villages and farms where their skills were required to patch leaking pots and pans, to render down old pewter into useful spoons, to collect scrap metal, or to make up any simple item required by their customers. If a carter wanted a piece of harness to be repaired, or a decorative rosette or face piece to be made for his horse, it is to these men that he would probably have turned.

The tools and equipment available to these metalworkers were quite simple, a hammer to flatten or form the metal, a saw, a pair of snips and a few files for shaping, a simple hand drill for piercing, and perhaps a graver or chasing tool with which to incise any decorative features. With these tools it would be quite easy to produce horse brasses possessing all the qualities of the earliest extant examples, although it must be stressed that handmade brasses need not necessarily date from before the popular introduction of cast brasses in the 1860s. Along the coast of the East Riding of Yorkshire, for example, handmade brasses are reputed to have been made up to the opening decades of the present century.

In contrast to the early stages of the decorative horse-brass industry, the production of saddler's and harness-maker's iron and brass accessories had been undertaken by a series of specialised craftsmen from the early Middle Ages at the latest, rowels, spurs and buckles often being made in quite separate workshops. By the 17th century a number of towns had acquired almost national reputations for the quality of their wares, one of the most important of these being Walsall, some ten miles north of Birmingham, in Staffordshire. Here as early as 1540, John Leland, the King's Antiquary, had noted the 'many smythes and bytte makers yn the towne' when compiling his great *Itinerary*. A further account of the Walsall trade was given by Dr Robert Plot in his *Natural History of Staffordshire* of 1686; the great period of expansion here took place in the late 18th and early 19th centuries, when the national growth of trade and industry brought with it an unprecedented demand for harness. Every movement of raw materials or manufactured goods across the country became dependent on horse power, thousands of these ideal draught animals being employed to haul enormous loads along the newly built turnpikes, canals, and railways. On the land the horse became increasingly important as the enclosure movement brought huge areas of wasteland and moorland under cultivation for the first time. The expansion of the Empire created similar requirements too, as the colonial farmers required extensive supplies of harness, as did the cavalry and artillery regiments of the vast British Army.

By the 1830s Walsall had become the recognised centre of the harness trade, numerous firms of fellmongers, tanners, curriers, brown and black saddlers and saddlers' ironmongers all gathering there to meet the demands of these expanding markets. In these circumstances it is hardly surprising that it was the Walsall founders who were responsible for the introduction of the first cast horse brasses about the middle of the last century. Already experienced in the making of bits, buckles and brass coach fittings, they were ideally equipped with the designers, pattern-makers and skilled workmen necessary for production.

When making a cast horse brass, an accurate drawing of the intended design is usually prepared, care being taken to ensure that it has as bold an outline as possible, for very thin sections or details on too fine a scale are bound to cause numerous faults in the eventual casting. The drawing has then to be transformed into a hard, three-dimensional pattern strong enough to leave a firm, clear impression in the casting sand. Some of the early patterns were carved directly from blocks of fine-grained wood, pear being particularly suited to this purpose. The majority were made either of lead or pewter, however, as these metals could easily be cast into shape and subsequently hand-finished to a high standard. In recent years Anthony Beebee Senior of Stanley Brothers, Walsall, made his patterns by modelling the required designs in plasticene on the back of a dinner plate. This was then covered in plaster of Paris, which set hard to form a negative mould into which molten lead was poured to make a positive pattern.

In addition to these single patterns, multiple patterns are now used whenever long production runs are required. They take the form of flat aluminium plates on which the raised patterns of each brass are joined to a series of strips which form the channels in the casting sand into which the molten brass is poured. By using these plates in conjunction

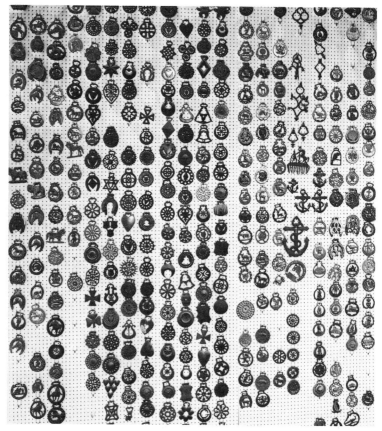

15. The Pattern Room, Stanley Brothers of Walsall.

with mechanical presses it is now possible to make a series of identical moulds much faster than ever before, with a consequent saving in both expense and trouble.

At the foundry of Stanley Brothers of Walsall brasses are still produced by the traditional tub-casting methods employed in the industry throughout the past century and a half. The process starts with a rectangular iron frame some two inches deep, known as a drag or 'she' mould from the two pierced lugs fixed on the outer edge of each of the longer sides. Placing the mould lugs upwards on a perforated iron plate laid on the casting bench, the caster fills it with dark red casting sand shaken through a wire sieve to remove any hard lumps. A mallet is then used to pound the sand into a firm cohesive mass, a steel straightedge scraping off the excess to leave a smooth, flat surface. Having dusted the surface

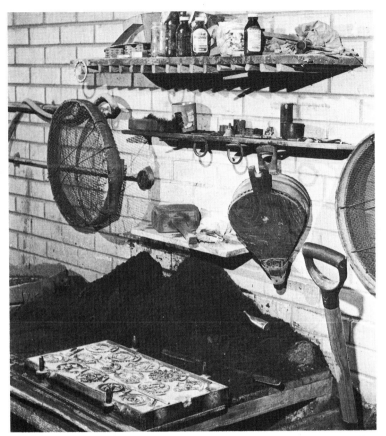

16. Casting Bench with the riddle, mallet, parting sand, bellows and straightedge.

with fine white casting sand contained within a small coarsely woven bag, the surplus is blown away with the hand bellows, thus leaving sand in an ideal condition to receive the impression of the patterns.

Next, three rows of four or five patterns are pressed face down into the sand so that their backs lie level with its surface, a small pellet of putty being used to connect each pattern to one of the two $\frac{1}{4}$-inch square brass rods which run longitudinally down the mould. These will eventually form the gates, or 'gets', down which the molten brass will flow. Having dusted the mould with casting sand once more, it is now extended upwards by the addition of the cope or 'peg' mould. This is identical in size to the drag or 'she', but has round tapered pegs which fit snugly into the pierced lugs of the mould below in order to ensure the exact register of one section with the other. Further casting sand is

17. (*Above, left*) Lifting the crucible from the furnace. 18. (*Above, right*)
Filling the moulds. 19. (*Opposite, top*) Knocking the sand from the brasses.
20. (*Opposite, bottom*) The cast brasses.

next sieved into the upper mould, being beaten down onto the patterns
and 'gets' to obtain a firm, clear impression. Once the surplus sand has
been scraped away, another perforated iron plate is placed over the
mould and the cope lifted free and inverted to reveal the negative
impression of the backs of the patterns, etc.

If only one mould is to be cast, the patterns can be lifted from the drag,
and the cope replaced to form brass-shaped cavities within the solid
block of sand. If continuous runs of brasses are being cast, however,
the caster leaves the patterns in place and proceeds to make a second
cope identical to the first. The whole mould, both cope and drag, is then
turned over and the first drag placed on top of the first cope. A second
drag is then made on top of the second cope, and so the process con-
tinues. In this way an indefinite number of moulds may be made without
having to repeat the troublesome rearrangement of the patterns and
gates.

Having completed the mould-making operation, the cope and drag
are firmly fastened together by means of strong iron clamps secured by
large wing nuts. They are then up-ended in rows against a low iron
platform, the entrances to the two gates being positioned on the top-
most edge. The caster then cuts off the flame in the furnace and swings

21. (*Top*) The brasses as they come from the mould.　22. (*Above*) A finely cast brass, complete with 'studs'.　23. (*Below*) Stamped pattern brasses. 24. (*Opposite, left*) Stamped designs: hearts, shields and stars.　25. (*Opposite, right*) Stamped design patterns.

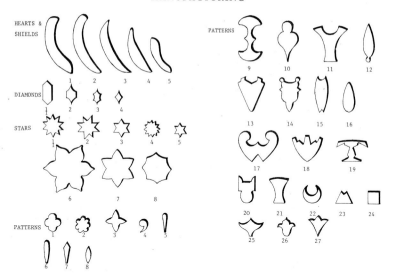

back the flue to reveal the glowing fireclay crucible in which the brass has been melted to a luminous golden liquid. Grasping the crucible with a pair of long, wide-jawed tongs, the caster spins it on its base across the floor to the awaiting moulds, where he lifts it on to the platform and skims off the slag with an iron bar into a tray below. The crucible is then rolled over to the first mould, where both gates are filled in turn, and so on until the whole batch is completed. Having been allowed to cool for a short while, the clamps are unscrewed, the iron plates removed, and the brasses knocked free, the sand falling away from their dull textured surfaces with a few taps of the mallet.

Up to the period of the First World War, cast brasses were usually provided with 'studs' or 'struts' – two narrow rods which projected perhaps ¾ of an inch from the back of each brass. These were formed by pricking a short spike or nail into the sand of the back face of the mould before the metal was poured. Their purpose was to provide a means of gripping the brass firmly in a vice so that it could be hand-finished, small files being used to reduce the rough-cast edges to a clean smooth outline. When handwork of this quality became too expensive, it was replaced by quicker, if cruder, techniques, an emery wheel removing the surplus brass in preparation for a final polishing on the buffing wheel.

As has been seen, the casting process was comparatively complicated and slow, each brass going through a number of labour-intensive stages

26. Coloured porcelain bosses with ornamental rivets.

before completion. Once the demand for horse brasses had become well established, the major manufacturers began to search for quicker and easier methods of production.

During the late 18th and early 19th centuries a number of new mechanical metalworking techniques were developed and readily adopted. The most important of these was the rolling of brass into thin sheets of uniform thickness, a great contrast to the hammered sheet of previous ages. This material could easily be cut to shape by specially made dies mounted in heavy fly presses, and so was ideal for making many items of small brassware.

Taking advantage of these developments, the manufacturers began to produce very large numbers of stamped brasses from the late 1870s or early 1880s. In the first operation, the brasses were punched out in

27. A mirror-brass in nickel.

outline, the blanks emerging as simple discs complete with integral hangers. These were then passed to individual craftsmen who worked at smaller presses equipped with numerous dies of various shapes and sizes, the most common being crosses, circles, crescents, dart and 'bat' shapes. Positioning each blank beneath the falling dies, the operator was enabled to build up pierced patterns of some complexity, the slight inaccuracies of the hand process giving a characteristic irregularity to the completed brass.

Most stamped brasses were basically two-dimensional but it was soon realised that designs could be raised in relief by embossing rather thinner sheet brass between specially made positive and negative dies. In this way, hemispherical domes, stepped cones and a series of decorative borders could be combined with the normal stamped decoration to

28. Stamped brasses showing a range of embossed designs.

produce an attractive range of pattern brasses. As a further development, the whole face of the brass could be stamped in relief, the flat areas within and around the raised details then being punched away completely. In this manner an effect very similar to that of cast brasses was achieved, but at a great saving of materials and labour. Horseshoes, shells and rearing horses were amongst the most popular designs to be produced in this manner.

Usually the brasses were sold in a plain, well-polished condition, but various decorations were sometimes added to give specially bright and colourful effects. The most popular of these were hemispherical porcelain bosses, their glossy surfaces showing either a solid mass of rich colour, such as royal blue or crimson, or bold concentric bands of contrasting hue. They were fastened back on to purposely made stamped brasses, the round or star-shaped head of the rivet appearing in the centre of each boss. Small discs of mirror could also be used in a similar way, their ornamental borders and central rosette motifs being carefully cut into the back surfaces of the glass before the silver coating was applied. In this way, each individual facet reflected the light, making it flash with every movement of the horse.

For special events, such as coronations or jubilees, photographs were sometimes mounted on brasses. On these occasions it was customary to produce thousands of small round pin-on badges showing sepia portraits of the famous figures of the day. It took but little ingenuity to stick these within the raised borders of stamped brasses in order to take advantage of the temporary boost in sales.

H. Robinson Carter owned a rectangular brass enclosing an illustration of Queen Victoria on the occasion of her 1887 Jubilee, but Edward VII was probably the first monarch to be popularly featured on photographic brasses. A review of William Overton's new designs in an early issue of *Saddlery and Harness* describes how 'some have real photographs of the King introduced, and mounted on brass or nickel. They are very effective. The price too is reasonable'.

From the opening of the present century through to the end of the First World War, ceramic enamels were occasionally used to provide areas of solid colour on the face of cast brasses, William Overton Limited of Walsall producing a range of patriotic designs employing this technique. The brass was first cast with flat-bottomed recessed areas wherever the colour was to appear, these then being filled with the pigment and subsequently heated to form permanent smooth, hard surfaces. When the use of these enamels was restricted to colouring in the various sections of a flag, for example, it could look quite well, but in some designs virtually the whole of the brass was submerged beneath the enamels, as may be seen in the shield-shaped tricolour 'peace and victory' brass of 1919 (*see* p. 39).

Brasses might also be decorated by the engraver, this craftsman being employed to cut inscriptions into otherwise standard pieces in order to meet some particular need. This was essentially a hand process as distinct from a mass-production technique. Having traced the proposed design on to the surface of the brass, he took it in his left hand and held it down firmly on to a leather pad stuffed with sand. He then took up the graver in his right hand, its lozenge or chisel-pointed blade extending to the tip of his thumb from a half-round wooden handle cradled deep within his palm. Using considerable controlled strength and skill, he proceeded to gouge out the design to the required depth, the form of the graver allowing him to vary the thickness of the lines to achieve the characteristic copperplate style. In most examples a rather plainer form of engraving was used, however, each letter being cut in plain sans-serif capitals, all their strokes being of an equal width.

A further method of decorating the brasses was borrowed from the high-class carriage harness trade. From the medieval period onwards the nobility and gentry had proudly displayed their crests on many parts of their travelling equipage. By the late 18th century a nobleman would have his state vehicles decorated with metallic crests nailed in a long row just below the roof line of his carriage, the same device appearing on the

29. (*Above*) A photographic brass showing George V, 1911.   30. (*Opposite, top*) Enamelled brasses made by William Overton Limited of Walsall.
31. (*Opposite, bottom*) Nickel details pinned on to brass backgrounds.

aiglets or sleeves of his footman, and also on the blinkers and side straps of his horses. To the naked eye, harness decoration of this quality appeared to be of solid silver, but this was an illusion.

Working from detailed drawings, and with reference to heraldic engravers' and painters' design books, such as Fairbairn's *Book of Crests*, the pattern-maker drew out the basic image in reverse on to a thin sheet of copper. This was then developed into three-dimensional form by a standard repoussé technique. A bowl of pitch, perhaps four to six inches in diameter, was heated until its contents had become soft and rather sticky. The sheet of copper was then firmly pressed into the surface of the pitch, where it stuck as the temperature dropped to normal. Then,

taking a variety of small steel punches, the pattern-maker beat the copper back into the yielding pitch in order to produce the negative form of the completed crest. This was an extremely skilful operation, the craftsman having to exert considerable judgement in shaping the crest, also having to avoid any heavy working which might fracture the thin copper sheet. Once satisfied that the internal shaping was completed, he then removed the metal from the pitch, turning it over to show the front face before pressing it back on to the pitch once more. In this position the contours of the modelling would be modified as required, and further detail added.

As it would have proved prohibitively expensive to have made each individual crest in this way, a simple method of producing extremely accurate duplicates was devised, this being the work of another craftsman known as the 'filler'. Taking the original pattern, he pressed it into bowls of warm pitch to leave a series of clear negative impressions. Into these he then pressed extremely thin sheets of brass, nickel or silver, a padded hammer enabling him to tap the sheet around all the smaller features. When these thin shells had been completed, they were then filled up with molten pewter, thin strips of tinned copper wire being inserted at this stage to reinforce any potentially weak areas, such as stag's antlers or horse's legs.

Having cooled, the filled shells then passed on to one of the most artistic of the foundry's craftsmen, the heraldic chaser. He mounted the shell face-upwards on a further bowl of pitch and proceeded to add all the finer details. Using small chasing tools resembling miniature chisels, he gave realistic textures to the fur, feathers, or scales, the rock or bark of the crests. Further conventional hatching (lines indicating shading) might also be added, its direction indicating the heraldic colour represented. This was often restricted to the six twists of the torque on which the crest stands.

Crests of this type were chiefly intended for use on carriage harness, but a number of armigerous families had them mounted on face pieces to be worn by their working horses on the farm. Crowns, royal heads and swingle-tree motifs were among other designs made in this way for the decoration of both face pieces and hame plates.

Throughout this volume the term 'brasses' has been constantly used when referring to the various pieces of metal horse decorations described. Most were of brass, it is true, but this was not the only metal to be used. German silver provided a suitable white-metal equivalent, while nickel was occasionally advertised as an alternative to brass for certain designs. It is interesting to consider H. Robinson Carter's suggestion that nickel 'brasses' had some connection with the fishing industry, for he had only come across them in Leith and Scarborough, further

32. The 'Queen's Silver Jubilee Horse', from Cleckheaton, West Yorkshire.

examples being reported to him as being used in Lowestoft (Carter, H. R. 'English Horse Amulets', *The Connoisseur*, Vol. LXV, 1916, p. 148). This might have been pure chance, but it is possible that they were more popular in coastal areas due to their higher degree of resistance to the sea mists. Nickel and brass were sometimes used together, as when bosses of one metal were mounted on 'brasses' of the other, or when the cast nickel coats of arms of the R.S.P.C.A. were pinned back on to their brass merit badges introduced in 1895. The R.S.P.C.A. was also responsible for the production of aluminium merit badges from the 1930s, their soft metal probably being easier to stamp or engrave with details of the award than any of the other metals available.

CHAPTER THREE

Collectors and Collecting

THE COLLECTING of horse brasses for their own sake, rather than as horse decoration, appears to have commenced around 1900. At that time the effects of industrialisation were becoming increasingly noticeable throughout England as towns expanded at an unparalleled rate, their sprawling suburbs swallowing numerous agricultural communities in their progress. Reacting against these changes, the middle classes began to adopt an idealised rural life-style typified by their cottagey country retreats, perhaps designed by Philip Webb, W. R. Lethaby or C. F. A. Voysey, and set in rich mellow gardens by Gertrude Jekyll. It was during this period that *Country Life* was founded (1897), the English Folk Song Society (1911), and the Folk Lore Society (1878).

Against this background, artistically minded ladies set out to collect horse brasses, partly in order to preserve them as part of the vanishing rural scene and partly to use them as decorations around the home. Writing in *Saddlery and Harness* in April 1911, a saddler told how:

I was considerably amused by the nature of a visit to my shop by two strange lady motorists. They wanted to know if I had any old brasses off old cart harness. They said they were collecting them as a hobby and were prepared to pay well for them, and also said they had many which were of 'really beautiful design'. New ones they would not have. I had nothing of the kind about, for all such old brass was promptly consigned to the old brass drawers and eventually to the cash till. I wonder how many other saddlers have had visits from these interesting ladies. It is surely the latest hobby extant. . . .

Further correspondents confirmed that a number of ladies had been collecting brasses for some years, using them as fingerplates on doors, or even mounting them back on to tin plates with putty, varnishing them, and hanging them on the wall as decorative plaques. It was even possible to stitch the brasses on to velvet or other material which was then sewn up and stuffed with sawdust to make an interesting bun-shaped pincushion. Later they became popular as decorative features on such costume accessories as belts, handbags, or hats, one lady appearing in the *Daily Mail* in the early 1930s wearing a pixie-shaped creation complete with five face pieces! In contrast to these rather frivolous collectors, Miss Lina Eckenstein provided the first serious study of the origin and purpose of horse brasses in a paper published in *The Reliquary and Illustrated Archaeologist* of 1906. Here she related her early attempt to form a collection of brasses, beginning by requesting old brasses from harness shops. As this method proved unsuccessful, due to the poor quality of the brasses available, she proceeded to make bids for those which were still in active use. This produced variable results, the farmer who had used them year in year out naturally proving reluctant to part with them, regardless of the sum offered. The carters were much more helpful, however, as they frequently pawned their brasses after the May-Day parade, or when they wanted to raise a few pence for a Saturday night out.

Having accumulated over 165 brasses (now preserved in the Ashmolean Museum, Oxford), Miss Eckenstein then proceeded to classify them by design, seeking to identify the most common motifs and trace them to their primary sources, always assuming they had been in continuous use from the earliest times. The crescent, she argued, was a lunar symbol of Stone Age origin, first being made up from a pair of curving boar's tusks bound together at their bases by a narrow thong or, as in the case of an example found at Wroxhall, Worcestershire, by an encircling metal band. Throughout India and Southern Europe the tips of the crescent had always pointed downwards, probably hanging from the binding around the tusks, but further north the tips had always pointed upwards, as they still tended to do in this country. Flat bronze decorations of this type found at Westhall in Suffolk and near the Roman camp at Ovington in Norfolk had probably hung from the mobile or breastbands of Roman cart-horses since identical features were shown on a memorial preserved in the antiquities department of the Römisch-Germanisches Museum in Cologne. Could these decorations be connected with the moon goddess Diana, patroness of hunting and chastity, and to whom horses were sacrificed?

The circular pattern brasses bearing radiant sun-burst motifs might well have a similarly ancient mythological origin, the sun being strongly associated with the driven horse. In India for example, the sun god was conveyed across the heavens in a car drawn by seven horses, while both the Scythians and the Rhodians sacrificed horses to the sun god. Even in Kent brasses were called 'sun brasses', thus stressing the continuity of this ancient belief.

The whorl originated from the fire kindled by rubbing wood on wood, and the heart from flint arrowheads, or from the Egyptians, which suggested a sacrificial connection. Although Miss Eckenstein's hypotheses do not bear close scrutiny, and leave an unaccountable space of some 2,000 years or more between the period of the beliefs and the appearance of the brasses, they did simulate considerable interest. What were horse brasses for, and what were their designs meant to represent?

At this point, Charles B. Plowright, the first male to join the written discussion, set out his views (Plowright, C. B. 'Suggested Moorish Origin of Certain Amulets in use in Great Britain', *The Reliquary*, New Series 12, 1906, p. 106). Having stressed his belief that harness amulets were chiefly used to avert the 'evil eye' and that their designs came down to us from the distant past, he went on to suggest that most of the common horse-brass symbols were Moorish. The crescent was certainly a popular Moorish motif, and became additionally significant when it enclosed an eight-pointed star, eight being a lucky number in Moorish magic. The fleur-de-lis, the shell and the quatrefoil could all be found in the decoration of the Alhambra, the palace of the Moorish kings at Granada in Spain. Even the two interlaced equilateral triangles known as the Seal of Solomon or the Star of David were to be found in Moorish art, although they might also be seen in the windows of Christian churches or on the vestment of the Dalai Lama of Tibet. Was it possible that these symbols had been brought into England by the crusader knights by way of the Moorish invasion of Spain, or even by the itinerant gypsies with their known fondness for horse decoration?

Unfortunately the theories expressed in these papers, both published in 1906, formed the basis of half a century's rather misguided suppositions regarding the mystic and symbolic aspect of horse brasses. Only in more recent years has any attempt been made to trace the history of brasses back from the present day, a study which soon indicated that they were introduced into this country in the late 18th century at the earliest, and had little connection with early civilisations. The opening decades of the present century were by no means wasted, however, for this was the classic period in which the first great collections were accumulated.

By 1911 E. V. Alison was able to describe his collection of 200 brasses, most of these being old cast examples (Alison, E. V. 'Brass Amulets', *The Connoisseur*, Vol. XXXI, 1911, p. 89). Prices were rising rapidly, face brasses of good design and workmanship now varying from 1s. (5p) to 4s. 6d. (22½p) each, whereas they had only cost a few pence a short time before. This sudden increase apparently encouraged disreputable dealers to 'fake' brasses for the collector's market, for some five years later H. Robinson Carter felt obliged to warn potential collectors of this deception (Carter, H. R. 'English Horse Amulets', *The Connoisseur*, Vol. LXV, 1916, p. 144):

They are easy to distinguish. The brass is much inferior in the modern specimens, and dirt is often burnt in at the back, so that they get a smooth appearance quite different to that of the genuine variety.

Carter's own collection was certainly of a very high quality, being built up in the opening decades of the present century. He was one of the most original and constructive writers on the subject, his articles published in *The Connoisseur* being the first to give a factual history of the horse brass, as opposed to the wildly conjectural accounts of his predecessors. Although a little reduced by fire damage, his collection still remains substantially intact in the Hull City Museums, and contains many fine and rare pieces.

About this time a further collection was being developed by Dr John L. Kirk, a doctor who lived and worked at Pickering on the southern edge of the North Yorkshire Moors. From the 1890s he had been gathering together a wealth of 'bygones' in order to preserve the every-day items of the past for the benefit of future generations. By 1931 he had over 400 horse brasses, a few more being added each month, in-cluding, for example, a Jubilee brass at 1s. 9d. (9p), a pair of brasses including Baden-Powell at 5s. (25p) each, and a Fred Archer brass which was acquired in January 1933. Some were collected locally, but the majority were obtained by advertising in national papers, such as the *Daily Independent* of 4 February 1933 (Manuscript records in the Castle Museum, York): 'Wanted, Fire Insurance Plates, Horse Brasses, Old Domestic and Personal Objects, Dr. Kirk, Pickering.' In 1938, his collection of some six hundred brasses was placed on display in his new museum, the Castle Museum at York, where they are still to be seen.

From the late 1930s, H. S. Richards, of Wylde Green, Warwickshire, provided a great service to the collector by publishing a series of small books illustrating some hundreds of brasses from the major British collections, in addition to a considerable number of his own. On his death, his collection passed to the Local History Department of Birm-ingham City Museums, where it is now stored. It includes brasses cast by the Period Brass Company, of which he was a director. These were taken from the brasses illustrated in his books and sold as reproductions at 10s. 6d. (52½p) per dozen.

Further significant collections were also formed about this time by C. Baillie Hamilton, Dr H. Leon Gauntless, A. Malaher, and Canon Hubert G. Stanley, whose collection, especially rich in fly terrets, was sold in 1943 for as little as £81. Probably the greatest collector of the years between the wars was a teacher at Charterhouse, A. H. Tod. At his home at 2, Prince's Buildings, Clifton, near Bristol, Mr Tod brought together over 1,100 different brasses, almost half of these being dis-played around his massive timbered fireplace. On his death in 1943, the whole collection was offered to Mr Richards for £1,000 (Manuscript records in the City Museum, Birmingham). Regrettably, he was unable to accept the offer so that it became necessary to split the collection

33. A stableman polishes a set of brass hames in the Harness Room at Ind Coope Breweries, St John Street, London. On the right is a single set made in 1931. The rest of the harness is of black leather on which are mounted decorations of brass barrels and laurel leaves. The martingales carry the 'hand' brasses, the Ind Coope trademark.

34. In the Harness Room of Scottish and Newcastle Breweries, the stableman polishes a high-bridged pad; the pad was made in Newcastle's Bigg Market in the early 1920s.

into lots and sell it off by auction on 18 February 1944. Fortunately, Mr Tod had supplied both Dr Kirk and Mr Richards with a series of photographs of his brasses some years before, and from these it is possible to gain a good impression of its quality. It included good ranges of armorial, commemorative and pattern brasses, hame plates and breast plates, as well as brasses featuring such West Country saddlers as Bell of Thomas Street, Bristol, and Banbury of Devizes.

Since the Second World War, a new generation of collectors has grown up, the renewed interest in horse brasses being reflected in the foundation of the National Horse Brass Society in 1975. Besides publishing an interesting and informative journal, *Horse Brass*, the society

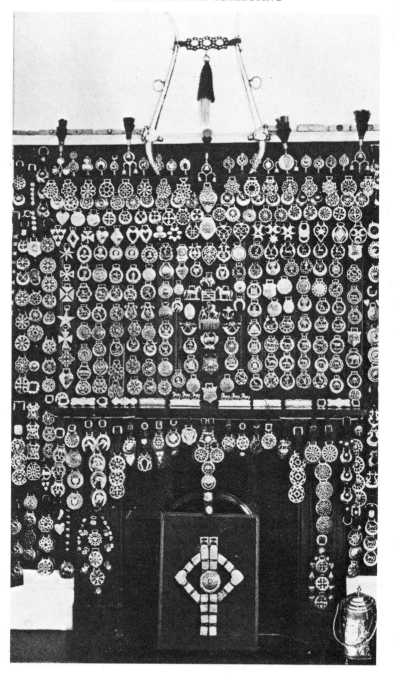

35. (*Opposite*) Part of Mr Tod's collection at Bristol.   36 (*Above*) A selection of Mr Tod's commemorative and heraldic brasses.

also arranges visits to notable collections and manufacturers, and issues a unique annual horse brass designed for members only. Certainly membership of this society is essential to all collectors, for it can provide one with a means of meeting others with similar interests, with details of forthcoming events, and with access to the most up-to-date information on every aspect of the horse brass.

It is interesting to consider why horse brasses provide such a popular field for the collector. Initially there is the appeal of the metal itself, its light golden colour and bright, highly reflective surface. Then there is

37. Manufacturing techniques: an old cast horse, a machine-cast 'Festival of Britain' brass, a stamped pattern brass and a stamped and embossed horse brass.

the quality of the workmanship, the fineness of the detail, the smooth finishing of the edges and lack of casting faults – the aesthetic quality too, the balance of the figurative detail with its surrounding border, or the overall cohesion of a design. For most people, however, the real attraction of horse brasses probably lies in their association with horses in rural transport and agriculture, for they certainly have the ability to evoke the most nostalgic elements of traditional country life.

To the purist, the only brasses worthy of collection are those made by hand or cast and hand-finished, generally before the First World War. They will also have been used for some years, and have an attractive soft patina acquired through constant wear and polishing. Brasses of this quality are now quite hard to find, however, and the greatest care

38. Back view of brasses opposite.

should be taken to discover if they are genuinely old. An early date or design provide no proof of this, for Queen Victoria Jubilee brasses bearing the date 1887 have been constantly reproduced since the late 1930s, for example, thousands being made for sale during the Silver Jubilee year of Elizabeth II in 1977.

In the case of handmade brasses, the collector should look for slight differences in the thickness of the metals, which should be cut from $\frac{1}{16}$-inch plate at least. The smooth back should show some indications of the hammering process used either to flatten, or, more commonly, to slightly raise the surface of the brass to a shallow convex form. When the edges of the brass are examined there should be little remaining evidence of either file or saw except in the tightest corners.

Old cast brasses exhibit a number of rather different characteristics, the most important of these being evident on the back face, where the dull, almost granular impression of the moulding sand still remains. To each side the bases of the studs should be seen, these being the remains of the narrow shafts by which the brass was gripped in the vice for hand-finishing. Once the finishing process had been completed, the studs were cut off, their truncated ends bearing the marks of the file or saw, unless they have been worn down to form soft, dome-shaped projections. Further evidence of hand-finishing may be seen by holding the brass up to the light, or by running the fingers around the perimeter of the design, when it will be found that all the rough edges have been filed down to present a smooth clean outline. It will also be noted that the edges of the design are slightly chamfered, this being a necessary feature of the original patterns in order to allow them to be lifted free from the casting sand with the least disturbance.

The backs of old brasses should also show areas where the metal has been brought to a dull, almost velvet-like smoothness due to the constant friction of the brass against the leather with every movement of the horse. This should be particularly noticeable around the lower edge of the brass, over the tips of the studs, and around the hanger, where considerable wear may have taken place. No file marks or areas of very high polish should be found in these parts, for these would show that the wear marks had been produced artificially in order to make the brass appear much older than it really is. When examining complete pieces of harness, such as breast plates, face pieces or straps, it is always worthwhile to check that the wear marks on the leather match those on the brasses, for new brasses can look very convincing when mounted on old harness, even though they might have come together quite recently. These guide lines for identifying old brasses, although quite accurate in themselves, cannot replace the almost instinctive 'feel' of an early brass which any collector may acquire with experience. Only by handling a number of genuinely old brasses can their qualities be fully appreciated; but even then the most experienced collector can make mistakes, for skilful fakes have now been made for well over 60 years.

Modern cast horse brasses, including most examples made after the end of the First World War when hand-finishing virtually ceased, may be identified by a number of characteristic features. From the front face, the lack of hand-finishing should be seen in the small sand textured excrescences which still remain around the edges of the design. Their presence is not conclusive, however, for hand-finishing was not always of the highest quality, as shown by the brasses illustrated by Lina Eckenstein in 1906, and now on view in the Ashmolean Museum, Oxford. The back face of the brass should provide more definite evidence of a recent date of manufacture, usually having a flat sand-textured surface lacking any trace of studs; the modern automatically packed moulds have one perfectly flat face. Where the traditional tub-casting methods are still in use, it is quite common for old brasses to be used as patterns, their truncated studs being faithfully reproduced on the back of the new brasses. They may still be readily distinguished from the old brasses, however, for the ends of their studs bear the imprint of the casting sand, as opposed to the clean-cut or worn ends of the originals.

As the demand for horse brasses grew towards the end of the 19th century, manufacturers began to introduce new, cheaper methods of production. The first of these was stamping, a thin sheet of machine-rolled brass being stamped out in outline, as a blank, and then ornamentally pierced by a number of small dies. These brasses are much lighter than the cast variety, and tend to take a rather finer polish, probably due to the burnishing effect of the process. On closely studying the face of the brasses it will be seen that the individual pierced motifs are not perfectly regular in their arrangement, their spacing and alignment varying with the skill of each operative as he positioned the brass under the falling punch. This irregularity is reminiscent of handmade brasses, but the uniform thickness of the brass, the lack of any hammer marks and the absence of any file or saw cuts around the edges confirm that they are stamped. On turning the brass over, it will be seen that the back surface is almost as smooth as the front, with none of the sand texturing found on cast brasses. If a finger is rubbed across the back, however, it will be noticed that the action of the punch has raised a short sharp ridge or arris round each perforation.

The same features are to be found on brasses which have been both stamped and embossed, although the arris can be rather harder to distinguish, perhaps because even thinner sheet metal had to be used where a high degree of relief was required.

Having learned the basic methods of horse-brass production and the characteristic features of the brasses themselves, the collector is likely to decide on a particular field of activity. If he has his own working horses he is sure to have very definite personal views on the quantity and quality of brasses his animals should wear, but most collectors will be primarily interested in the pleasures of acquiring their specimens, and in the decorative effect their brasses will produce in the home. Seventy years ago it was possible to build up magnificent general collections of good quality, but this is hardly the case today. Handmade brasses are very rarely seen, and are hardly ever offered for sale, but old cast and punched brasses are still available. The new collector will probably wish to purchase almost every old brass that comes his way through local antique shops, salesrooms or farm auctions, but he may then decide

39. Souvenir brasses from York.

to specialise, selling or exchanging his spares to obtain others of particular interest.

There are many fruitful areas in which the collector may concentrate,
face pieces offering the greatest variety. The major sections include
animals, heraldic devices, horses and horsehoes, farming subjects,
awards, abstract patterns, commemorative and company brasses, such
as those used by breweries or railway companies. Stamped face pieces
can be particularly interesting, too, identical punches often being used
in a number of different designs. Souvenir brasses represent one area
where relatively little interest has been shown to date, largely due to
their comparatively recent appearance, and the fact that they were made
for tourists rather than for horses. Even so, some satisfactory designs
have been produced, many featuring famous people and places. They

certainly provide the most inexpensive means of starting a collection, besides serving their intended function as attractive souvenirs. Hames, hame plates, and saddler's brasses offer further possibilities, as do bells, fly terrets, flower vases, or other more specialised items of harness decoration.

Even with quite a small collection, it can be very difficult to remember the features of each brass, a problem which proves quite troublesome when considering the purchase of further specimens. An efficient and practical solution was developed by Dr Kirk in the 1920s, when he prepared a small photograph of each section of his collection, these being mounted on card and hinged together to form a long zigzag strip which concertinaed neatly into his vest pocket. Using this reference to show some 400 brasses, he was able to avoid spending his money on expensive duplicates instead of those he really wanted.

Having acquired a brass, further information regarding its origins may be obtained from a number of different sources. Some of the most interesting of these are the trade catalogues published by the manufacturers and wholesalers of horse furniture and issued to the retailers in order to promote sales. They are beautifully illustrated with engraved or lithographed drawings showing every detail of harness and its decoration, including all the brasses they produced. One of the earliest to show face pieces was published in 1883 by Matthew Harvey of Walsall, this being followed in later years by *A Pattern Book of Harness and Carriage Mountings* of Thomas Crosbie of Birmingham of *c.* 1885, *The Equine Album* by Thompson and Scott of the Clarence Works, Walsall in the 1890s, the various editions of *The Saddlers' Red Book* by William Overton & Company, of Freer Street, Walsall, and *Four in Hand* by R. E. Thacker & Company of Walsall, 1895 and 1905. These catalogues are now extremely rare, and it is likely that collectors will find it quite difficult to obtain copies for study. However, a good selection has been published by Terry Keegan in his *Scrapbook of Harness Decorations*, while a number of pages from various catalogues are reproduced in each issue of *Horse Brass*, the journal of the National Horse Brass Society. It must be noted that the appearance of a particular design in a catalogue need not imply that it was produced solely by that manufacturer, for some of the most popular designs were common to most makers while the pirating of designs from one firm to another was not unknown. A greater degree of certainty is possible when pattern numbers can be compared for each drawing was referenced by a pattern number to facilitate ordering. This number was frequently cast into the backs of the brasses, although stamped brasses were usually left unnumbered, making identification a little more difficult.

In addition to the pattern number, other identification marks may also

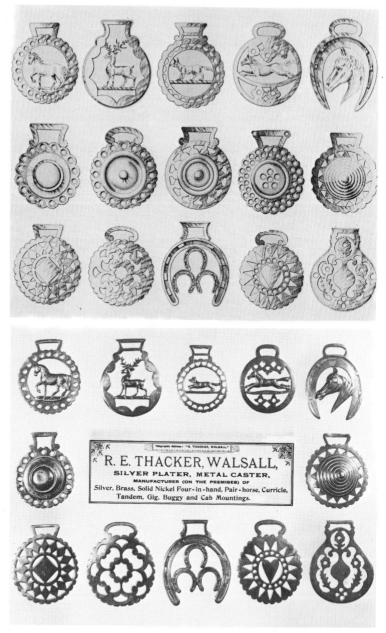

40. (*Top*) A page from Thacker's *Four in Hand* catalogue, 1895.   41. (*Bottom*)
Brasses featured in Thacker's 1895 catalogue.

42. Baden Powell, 'Rd. No. 357452'.

be found on the backs of the brasses. Between 1842 and 1883 it was possible for manufacturers to obtain protection for their designs by enrolling them in a central registry. A diamond-shaped registration mark was then inscribed on each protected item, a series of code letters within the diamond indicating the material of which it was made, the date of the design, and a reference to the registry office records containing further detailed information. In 1883 the form of registration was changed, the diamond mark being replaced by the registered number, a consecutive number being given to each design from number one, issued in that year. The date of the numbered registered design can be obtained from the tables printed on page 123.

Occasionally the brass might also bear a maker's mark, but these are comparatively rare, the most common being the 'w.o.w.' cast into the backs of the later brasses made by William Overton of Walsall. Even rarer are those stamped with their owner's name, for the brasses were usually the property of the waggoner, rather than his employer, except in the case of the larger companies and corporations. One of these, a stamped face piece, is recorded with the mark '. . . c. WALL' punched on to its face, this being the mark of J. C. Wall, carriers for the Great Western Railway.

CHAPTER FOUR

Horse Brass Designs

WHILE THE previous chapters cover the development and manufacture of horse brasses, the present chapter sets out to describe the various designs employed in their decoration. It cannot hope to be exhaustive, for there are probably over 2,000 extant designs, but it can define the main varieties and suggest their probable origins.

AWARD AND MERIT BADGES

Towards the end of the 19th century there was a great movement to improve the conditions of the thousands of working horses which provided the motive power on all Britain's roads. In the metropolis the London Cart Horse Parade Society was founded in 1885, its first parade on Whit Monday, 1886 proceeding around Regent's Park and on to King's Cross. Four years later the competition was opened to all drivers operating within seven miles of Charing Cross; prizes were awarded to those drivers whose horses and harness were in the best condition. The Royal Society for the Prevention of Cruelty to Animals worked closely with the Parade Society, and in 1895 issued their first award brasses, which were shield-shaped with a cast nickel royal coat of arms pinned just beneath the hanger and the inscription 'MERIT BADGE OF R.S.P.C.A. GIVEN AT LONDON CART HORSE PARADE' together with the date. These were made both in brass and aluminium in the 1930s, being replaced with a plastic material shortly after the war. (For further information see Bradbury, Derrick, 'Merit Badges and Parade Awards', *Horse Brass 4*, p. 6, and Follett, Ken, 'R.S.P.C.A. Merit Badges', *Horse Brass 1*, p. 17.)

The year 1904 saw the introduction of the London Van Horse Parade for smaller horses; the R.S.P.C.A. presented merit badges on this occasion from 1907 (their design being similar to those used for the Cart Horse Parade) to 1939 (when a horseshoe shape was adopted). This was last issued in 1965 when the Van Horse Parade Society and the Cart Horse Parade Society amalgamated to form the Harness Horse Society which has continued to issue its own horseshoe-shaped award brasses ever since.

In addition to the shield-shaped brasses issued at the London parades, the R.S.P.C.A. awarded round brasses, bearing similar nickel coats of

43. Animals: the Arabian and Bactrian camels, boar, squirrel, cat and cow.

arms and inscriptions, at other shows throughout the country. Our Dumb Friends League, later known as The Blue Cross, also awarded brasses during their campaign to ban the docking of horse's tails. These were of die cast bronze or nickel and showed a horse with a flowing tail and a broad-armed cross inside a round border, inscribed 'OUR DUMB FRIENDS LEAGUE / BEST UNDOCKED HORSE', the brass itself having an octagonal outline. The People's Dispensary for Sick Animals' award brass was stamped from lightweight brass, the initials 'P.D.S.A.' being fretted out above the inscription 'AWARD / PRESENTED BY THE / PEOPLES DISPENSARY / FOR SICK ANIMALS / PATRON THE PRINCE OF WALES'.

Further merit badges were presented by a number of local cart horse parade societies mainly established in the south-eastern counties around the turn of the century. Most of them copied the shield shape of the London R.S.P.C.A. badges, but the royal arms were replaced by a more suitable device. Westminster, Lambeth and Southwark used their borough arms, for example, while Walsall used its town badge, the Bear and Ragged Staff of the Earls of Warwick.

ANIMALS

The Antelope The antelope is one of the Queen's Beasts, having served as the badge of Henry V and Henry VI. It is distinguishable from the stag by its short round horns which, according to Thomas Bewick, 'are remarkable for a beautiful double flexion, which gives them the appearance of the lyre of the ancients'.

The Bear The bear appears in a number of different forms on horse brasses, sometimes standing with its four feet on an heraldic torque, or else in the act of dancing upright within a round scallop-edged border. Bears have been imported into England from at least the mid 13th century when one was kept by Henry III in the Tower of London, a strong cord being provided to hold him whenever he bathed in the Thames. Up to the period of the First World War dancing bears toured the country towns where they performed various antics in response to the pipe or organ music provided by their masters. As an early 19th-century writer commented:

The bears are made to stand upon hot iron and undergo the severest discipline before they are fit for public exhibition, a truth which harrows the feeling and makes me wish the dancing bears unmuzzled, and let loose on those who have the guidance of their education!

The dancing bears also wrestled with a wooden pole as part of their act, the Bear and Ragged Staff becoming the badge of the Earls of Warwick. This device appears on a number of brasses, often being placed on top of the Staffordshire Knot, the combination thus formed being the badge of the town of Walsall. It can be seen on the Founder Member's brass issued by the National Horse Brass Society in 1975.

The Boar The boar became a popular design for inn signs in the medieval period, being the badge adopted by King Richard III, while in more recent heraldry it appears complete in the punning arms of the Bacon, MacSwynie and Swinhoe families, the head alone being used by the Piggs, Swinburns and Swynesheads.

The Bull The Bull, the Bull's Head or the Bull and Grapes were frequently used for inn signs and are shown on a number of horse brasses. The bull usually stands on a flat strip of rough ground, but may also be found with the head only mounted on a torque as a crest.

The Camel, Arabian and Bactrian These animals are distinguished by their single and double humps, respectively. The first usually stands within a circular scalloped border edged with pierced semicircles, while the second is seen within either a pear-shaped frame scalloped around its inner edge, or a simple round border scalloped around its outer edge.

The Cat Horse brasses illustrating cats were first produced early this century (but before 1916) when a whole series of farmyard animal designs began to appear. The cats are seated upright, their tails wrapped around their front paws. Manx cats, meanwhile, stand with their four

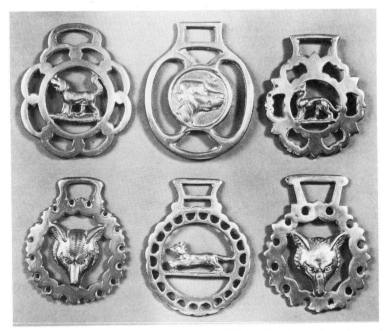

44. Dogs and foxes, with a talbot, a spaniel's head and a greyhound.

paws on an heraldic torque, and are easily recognised by the lack of a tail.

The Cow The cow was one of the farmyard subjects produced early this century, and is usually shown within a circular border deeply notched round the perimeter.

Dogs Most of the dogs found on horse brasses have good heraldic pedigrees, originating with the talbot, or hunting dog, and the greyhound. The talbot was particularly popular, reflecting its punning appearance on the arms of the powerful family of Talbot, Earls of Shrewsbury, and its consequent use on inn signs wherever they were influential. Both talbots and greyhounds, either on foot, seated or with their heads in profile, are shown on heraldic torques, within a variety of borders. One of the rarest and most beautiful designs shows the talbot running across a horizontal panel of scrolling foliage modelled in relief, the whole being mounted on a six-leafed Tudor rose border.

A further design bears the head of a spaniel modelled in relief on a round medallion within a plain round border. Toby, the small terrier associated with Punch and Judy, is also commemorated as a brass, being easily recognised by his feathered hat and clown's ruffled collar.

The Donkey Like the cow, the donkey was one of the farmyard sub-

45. Elephants, including 'Jumbo' and 'Alice'.

jects introduced early this century. It is found standing on an area of rough grass within a quatrefoil opening in a round brass.

Elephants In the 1860s, visitors to London Zoo were always sure to see its most famous inhabitant, Jumbo the elephant, together with his consort, Alice. Articles about him were printed in the popular press, he was modelled in Staffordshire pottery, and inspired a number of horse brasses. The most common design shows him freestanding, his feet squeezed tightly on to a small half round base inscribed 'JUMBO'. He also appears (a) freestanding in a more natural pose, his legs quite vertical,

(b) in a similar stance within a round border with a scalloped outer edge, or (c) within a round, scallop-edged border pierced with semicircular holes.

Alice appears on a single brass, within a round, scallop-edged border pierced with round holes and inscribed 'ALICE'. The couple was split up on Jumbo's sale to the American Barnum and Bailey's Circus, leading to popular songs, such as the following:

> Jumbo said to Alice 'I love you'.
> Alice said to Jumbo 'I don't believe you do,
> If you really loved me as you say you do,
> You would not go to Yankeeland and leave me in the Zoo'.

The Fox The role of hunting in the English countryside was sufficiently important to ensure that the fox would be included in any expression of folk art. He is seen (a) standing in a plain round border, (b) running across the brass surrounded by a round scalloped border pierced with semicircles, (c) while his mask, with delicately pointed nose and ears, appears within round borders which have either pierced inner circlet, or (d) an elaborately cast twelve-lobed fleurs-de-lis design.

The Griffin This fabulous creature, with eagle's head and wings on the body of a lion, is popular in heraldry, being best known as the central device on the Welsh flag. On brasses, it is found squatting on its haunches, one claw holding erect a small shield, the round border being edged with sixteen fleurs-de-lis motifs. Alternatively, the body and forequarters of the griffin may rise from a torque within a round scallop-edged border pierced with semicircles.

The Hare The hare does not appear on old brasses, being a relatively modern design. It is seen lying down, ears erect, within a round scalloped-edged border.

The Hedgehog The hedgehog is usually seen in profile standing on a strip of brass within a zigzag-edged round border.

The Horse For obvious reasons, this is by far the most popular of all figure brasses. The horse is most often seen in a walking pose within borders of almost every type, including one made up of eight forelegs arched over a similar number of horseshoes. A further design shows a galloping horse, its limbs at full stretch and its tail flowing behind as it flies across a circular brass decorated with five small pierced trefoils. The prancing horse may owe its origin to the White Horse of Hanover which appeared on the royal arms of England from the reign of George I to that of William IV, or to the Kentish 'Invicta', the prancing horse which is the symbol of that county. This is certainly one of the liveliest of horse-brass designs, the movement of the horse usually being represented quite beautifully by the modeller. Brasses showing horses in this stance

46. Cast horses.

were often produced by stamping rather than by casting, one type showing a prancing horse raised in relief on a flat scalloped disc of brass, while in the other the background of the horse was cut away to leave it standing inside the rounded moulding of the border.

Horses are also depicted wearing harness, the most common showing a freestanding heavy horse in trace harness, with blinkered bridle, collar, back and hip straps, and trace chains. These are made in two versions with the horse facing either to the right or to the left, allowing them to be made up symmetrically if required. Full shaft harness is shown in at least three designs, each animal being furnished with a cart saddle, belly band, and heavy breechings in addition to the bridle and collar. Horses equipped in this way are found either modelled in relief inside (a) a round scallop-edged border, (b) inside a round sixteen-lobed fleurs-de-lis border, or (c) within a horseshoe, or (d) inscribed in outline into a nine-lobed circle of brass, the latter design frequently appearing on matching hame plates too.

The horse's head may be mounted as a crest on an heraldic torque inside a round sixteen-lobed fleurs-de-lis border, but this type is quite unusual. Most designs frame the head, either in profile or in a three-quarters view within a horseshoe, an arrangement common both to cast and stamped brasses. Only two designs show the full frontal aspect of

47. (*Left*) Stamped horses.   48. (*Right*) Free-standing horses.

the head. In the first, a single head bridges a pierced quatrefoil in an otherwise plain round brass, while in the second the head is surrounded by twelve similar heads which form a radiating border.

The Kangaroo This most unusual subject was probably introduced early this century for the colonial market. The kangaroo is seen squatting on its haunches within a round scalloped border pierced by fifteen round holes.

The Lion The qualities of the lion are inflamed, according to Thomas Bewick, 'by influence of a burning sun, its rage is most tremendous, and its courage undaunted'. With these attributions it is easy to see why the lion became one of the most important heraldic devices of the Middle Ages, featuring in the royal arms of England, Scotland, Norway, Sweden, Hungary, Austria, Belgium, Holland, Luxemburg, Bavaria, Spain, Bohemia, and so on.

On brasses, he usually adopts the rampant pose, standing in profile on one hind paw, the other three being raised in attack. He is also seen passant, that is walking along and looking straight to the front; as a demi-lion, issuing waist-up from a torque; or merely as a mask, his head fringed by a long shaggy mane. In these forms he appears in many brasses, with or without a torque, and in a great variety of borders.

The Monkey This brass shows a chained ape on all fours within a

49. A pride of lions.

circular border, and may have originated from the organ-grinder's monkey so popular in mid-Victorian England. An heraldic origin is also possible, however, for this device formed part of the arms of the Marmion family, and is now the crest of the Dukes of Leinster. According to a family tradition, the infant Earl of Kildare was accidentally left behind in the Castle of Woodstock when it caught fire. Although his room was completely destroyed, it was discovered that a pet monkey had broken loose and carried the child to safety, the Earl later adopting the monkey and its broken chain as his crest.

Pegasus Pegasus, the winged horse of Greek mythology, sprang from the blood which sank into the ground when Perseus cut off the head of Medusa. Minerva, Goddess of Wisdom, caught and tamed him before presenting him to the Muses; later he caused the Hippocrene fountain on Mount Helicon to flow by the stroke of his hoof. To the carter, however, the winged horse most probably signified lightness and speed. He is depicted as a crest, flying either above a torque on a circular scalloped-edged brass bordered with alternate pierced triangles and semicircles, or within a round border edged with sixteen fleurs-de-lis.

The Pig and the Sow These subjects form part of the farmyard series introduced early this century.

Stag and Deer The use of the stag as a decorative and symbolic device was already well established by the medieval period, when it began to be

50. Saddler's brasses.

51. Pegasus and a unicorn.

employed in heraldry. From this source the stag was incorporated into horse-brass designs, most being modelled on the engraved illustration in volumes such as Fairbairn's *Book of Crests*. The stag is most often seen in profile, walking to the left, or appearing 'couchant', that is, lying down with its body resting on its legs, and its head held erect. Its head is also shown separately, mounted on an heraldic torque.

The female deer, or hind, bears no antlers, but its head forms the graceful crest of Whitbreads, the brewers, and is used on their harness.

The Squirrel Another of the farmyard series, the squirrel squats on its haunches as it nibbles at a nut clasped in its paws. It is found within a variety of borders.

The Unicorn With its horse's body, goat's beard, lion's tail, and the long single horn sprouting from its forehead, the unicorn was an awesome beast. Having supported the royal arms of Scotland for centuries, the unicorn was incorporated in the royal arms of England on the accession of James I in 1603. It is usually shown passant, walking to the left with its right front hoof raised and its tail curving over its back, a formal, yet lively, pose within its round border edged with sixteen fleurs-de-lis. A further version lacks both the beard and the lion's tail, and appears to be a mere horse converted into a unicorn by the simple addition of a horn to the old pattern. This design stands within a plain round border.

Birds

The Cock Designs showing the cock probably originated from heraldic sources, although the farmyard rooster would form a popular subject for the carter in its own right. The cock stands on a narrow strip of brass within a round border either plain, scallop-edged and pierced with fourteen round holes, smooth-edged and pierced with semicircles, or made up of thirteen pierced circles. One brass illustrated in fig. 296 of H. S. Richards' *All About Horse Brasses* shows a pair of game cocks fighting within a round scalloped border inscribed '18.C.COX.35', the theme punning the owner's name. The pictorial quality of the modelling and the character of the lettering prove that this brass is far more recent than the inscription would suggest, a 1930s date being much more likely.

The cock is also found standing on a bugle mounted over an heraldic torque, all within a plain round border.

The Duck This design is one of the farmyard series produced early this century.

The Eagle The eagle appears on relatively few brasses, considering its extensive use in heraldry, and as the symbol of imperial Rome, Napo-

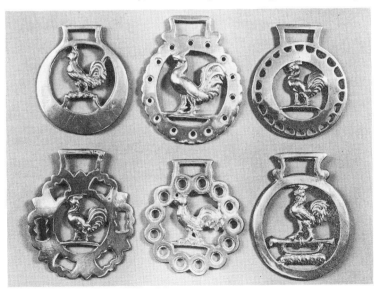

52. A selection of cock brasses.

53. The eagle, owl and partridge with a falcon and phoenix.

leon, and the United States of America. It is difficult to define a typical pose for this bird, for it is found with wings outstretched, stooping, standing upright, or issuing from a torque. In one design it is seen from a three-quarters viewpoint, its head turned back to peck at a bunch of grapes dangling from a vine, all within a plain round border.

The Emu This design was produced early this century, presumably for use in the colonies. The bird stands on a naturalistic background within a scallop-edged border pierced by semicircular holes.

The Falcon One of the Queen's Beasts, being the badge of Edward III, the falcon probably became a horse-brass design through the influence of heraldic source books.

The falcon is seen within a scallop-edged round border pierced with semicircles, its wings extended upwards as if it were just about to take flight.

Love Birds Love birds form an unusual subject in English folk art, being much more common in the countries of northern Europe. They are found in one design, however, standing bill to bill within an oval scrolled cartouche joined to the plain round border by four curving supports.

The Magpie This design appears to be one of the farmyard series introduced early this century.

54. A selection of 'brasses' made of nickel.

The Ostrich Like the emu, this bird was probably designed for use in the colonies some time between the First and Second World Wars.

The Owl The owl is well known in heraldry, its use on the arms of the Savile family of West Yorkshire leading to its inclusion as supporter to to the arms of the City of Leeds, where owl brasses are said to have been popular. The owl sits in profile, its head turned towards the viewer, within a round scallop-edged border pierced by either semicircular or round holes.

The Partridge Along with the fox and the hare, the partridge owed its popularity to the sporting interests. It is seen walking across a flat strip within a pear-shaped border scalloped around its inner edge.

The Peacock The peacock has often been regarded as an unlucky bird, even the ownership of one of its feathers being considered unwise, and so it is rather surprising to find it in some nine horse-brass designs. In six of these, it is shown 'in its pride', full-faced with its tail opened so as to fill almost the entire area within its border. Further brasses show the peacock in profile, its tail resting on the ground, while another version shows it walking to the right, its tail extending so far to the left that the border has had to be pulled into a horizontal pear-shaped form in order to accommodate the whole bird. This is surely one of the weakest and most ill-balanced designs ever to have been produced as a horse brass.

The Pelican The 'Pelican in her Piety' is a well-known subject in medieval art, frequently appearing in carved oak beneath the misericord seats of the choir stalls, for example. According to legend the pelican pecked blood from her own breast in order to feed her young, symbolic of Christ's blood being spilled for the benefit of mankind. It is thought likely that the legend grew up from a mistaken observation of a flamingo ejecting a secretion of blood from its mouth, for the pelican behaves quite normally in regard to the care of its chicks.

The pelican is found in at least two horse-brass designs. In the first, she stands upright, with wings extended and her neck gracefully arched so that her long beak rests against her breast, all within an elaborate shield-like border. In the second, she stands in a similar pose above her nest, which holds four chicks, this motif being mounted on a torque within a round seventeen-lobed fleurs-de-lis border.

The Pigeon or Dove Although the dove is a well known Christian device, also being the personal symbol of St David, patron saint of Wales, the origin of this design cannot be accurately traced. It might have been based on an illustration in an heraldic volume, in a natural history publication such as Thomas Bewick's *History of British Birds*, or on the personal observation of the modeller. It is seen facing left in profile within a six-petalled rose border.

The Phoenix This mythical bird, the only one of its kind, lived for five or six centuries in the Arabian desert before burning itself on a funeral pyre, only to arise again with renewed youth and vigour to live through a further cycle. For obvious reasons, it was adopted as the symbol of the Phoenix Assurance Company, being stamped in relief on to metal plaques supplied to their policy holders. These were then nailed to the outside of the insured building to inform the local fire brigades that they would be paid by the company should they help to extinguish a fire there.

On horse brasses, the phoenix is seen in a three-quarters pose emerging from the flames with outstretched wings, the round border being divided

55. The pelican, the 'Pelican in her Piety', and two swan brasses.

into shallow 'teeth' around its outer edge, very much like a gear-wheel.

The Swan The swan is a well known heraldic device, appearing as the badge of Henry V, and on the arms of the Staffords, Dukes of Buckingham, thus being adopted on to the arms of the Borough of Buckingham and Buckinghamshire County Council. It is usually shown as if it was swimming to the left, within a round scallop-edged border pierced with semicircles.

73

INSECTS

The Bee Symbolising industry, the bee appears on a single horse-brass design, being viewed from above with its wings and legs arranged symmetrically about a vertical axis. The round scallop-edged border is pierced by seven round holes.

The Grasshopper The grasshopper of the Gresham family still stands over the Royal Exchange in London, and is found on a single horse-brass design.

56. Windmills and towers.

BUILDINGS

Towers One horse-brass design shows a castle in some detail, a large round tower on the left being defended by a pair of smaller towers to the right, all within a plain round border. This is reputed to be the Tower of Refuge in Douglas Bay on the Isle of Man, presumably having been made for the tourist market during the inter-war years. The 'Lewes Castle' design shows a symmetrical gothic facade with a central arched gateway flanked by two battlemented towers, all on a raised mound within a round scallop-edged border. Since it was described by the earliest collectors, it is likely that this brass was first produced in the late 19th century.

A further brass shows a round building with a four-arched porch and four receding storeys, each one having an arched colonnade around its perimeter. It has been called the Colosseum, the Crystal Palace, the former Royal Exchange, the Albert Hall, or the Tower of Babel. Unfortunately, it does not resemble any of these with any degree of accuracy, although it tends to have much in common with contemporary biblical prints showing the latter subject. It usually appears within a plain round border with an additional horizontal bar across the hanger.

The Statue of Liberty This design was first advertised about 1944 by H. S. Richards' Period Brass Company at 3s. 9d. (19p) each. The statue

57. A selection of colourful brasses issued for the Silver Jubilee of Her Majesty Queen Elizabeth II in 1977. Royal celebrations such as coronations and jubilees are popular themes for horse brasses.

58. The cross and cross-crosslet brasses.

stands within a round border, with short scrolls springing from the bottom ends of the hanger.

The Windmill One of the farmyard series, the usual designs show either (a) a round tower mill with the four sails set diagonally and facing the viewer, the scallop-edged round border being pierced by seven round holes, or (b) a similar mill, with the addition of a gallery, in a plain round border.

Christian Subjects

The Cross Although there are a number of designs incorporating heraldic crosses, the Christian cross, with narrow parallel-sided arms, is extremely rare. Two versions are represented in the H. Robinson Carter collection at Hull. In the first, the cross is pierced through a circular brass, thirteen round holes being cut through the remaining four quarters. In the second, the pierced cross lies in the centre of a four-petalled flower, small diagonal leaves filling the spaces between each petal.

The Flight into Egypt This brass shows a camel walking across the desert, a child sitting in the crook of its neck, a woman on the hump, and a man walking behind, these supposedly representing the Christ child, Mary and Joseph on their flight into Egypt. The round border is perforated with six circles and a lozenge shape, the whole design probably being introduced during the inter-war years.

The Lamb and Flag The Agnus Dei, or Lamb of God, stands passant, its right foreleg holding the shaft of a red crossed banner which is seen over its shoulder, the small erect head being haloed. This symbol has been widely used by the church from the early medieval period, and is recorded on a single horse-brass design, encircled by a broad scallop-edged border pierced with a circle of small round holes.

Noah's Ark On the brass, the ark is seen floating on the flood, while a row of animals promenade along the deck, the narrow round border having a scalloped outer edge. This design was probably introduced between the First and Second World Wars largely for the collector's market.

St Andrew St Andrew, the Galilean fisherman who became Christ's first apostle, was crucified on an X-shaped cross according to a late medieval version of his life. He is the patron saint of Scotland, his white cross saltire on a blue ground being the Scottish flag. This brass shows the robed saint holding his cross with both hands, the surrounding border being of an elaborate shield shape.

St Blaise's Comb St Blaise, or Bishop Blaise as he was better known in England, was Bishop of Sebaste in Armenia, being martyred in A.D. 316 by being torn with iron wool combs. He thus became patron saint of wool-combers, also acquiring a posthumous reputation for healing cattle, stoppages of the throat and toothache. On the continent decorative horse brasses in the form of blunt-toothed Bishop Blaise's combs were frequently attached to the collar. Some were stamped from sheet brass, one example from Rothenburg in Bavaria, which can be seen in the Pitt-Rivers Museum in Oxford, is stamped '1877 / LEON HALL : SCHLEIR / IN BOFENSENTEILER' within a border of overlapping impressed circles.

Further examples from Meran in the Tyrol show either a symmetrical pair of prancing horses, or a rearing horse being restrained by a man in a mid 19th-century costume, complete with top boots, breeches and riding coat. This particular design is occasionally found in England, A. H. Tod having acquired one from an old horseman, while an identical pattern still exists at Stanley Brothers Foundry in Walsall.

St George The figure of St George, patron saint of England, is seen on horseback, trampling the dragon which writhes beneath the flailing hooves. This design was copied from that of a gold sovereign.

Commemorative: Events

The Boer War 1900 In *Saddlery and Harness* for April 1900, William Overton Limited of Walsall advertised 'The Newest thing in hanging plates, fly terrets and rosettes, National Flags in Colour – on brass or nickel' while two months later an editorial article was able to say:

The patriotic horse ornaments introduced and registered by W. Overton Ltd. have had an enormous sale, catching on as they did just in time for the demonstrations celebrating the relief of Ladysmith and Mafeking.

These particular brasses take the form of slightly domed discs with scalloped edges, their faces having sunken panels into which the coloured enamels were introduced. One of the designs shows the Union Jack flying from a mast, another, the Union Jack crossed with a striped red, white and blue flag and the date '1900'. Both are marked 'REGD' on the front, and 'w.o.w.' on the back.

The Entente Cordiale 1904 A further William Overton enamelled design showing the Union Jack crossed with the tricolour probably commemorates the signing of the Anglo-French agreement of 18 April 1904.

Peace and Victory 1919 Also by William Overton, this brass takes the shape of a flat banner of vertical red, white and blue stripes across which a flowing scroll reads 'VICTORY'. A further scroll across the top of the banner is inscribed 'PEACE/1919' while the bottom is modelled as a deep fringe.

Tutankhamun 1922 A suite of six brasses were cast in Egyptian designs in 1922 to commemorate the discovery of the tomb of Tutankhamun. The full set of patterns are still held by Stanley Brothers, and comprise five Egyptian heads, plus one of a lioness-headed god.

The Victory Brass 1945 Designed by H. S. Richards, this brass has the Victory 'v' within a garter scroll inscribed '1939 . VICTORY . 1945', all within a laurel wreath, the classical emblem of the victor. Specimens were accepted by the Prime Minister, Field-Marshal Montgomery and General Eisenhower in July 1945, following which they were offered for general sale at 5s. (25p) each.

The Festival of Britain 1951 These face pieces bear the inscription 'FESTIVAL OF BRITAIN 1951' on a flat round border surrounding the Festival symbol, a classical helmeted head springing from the three compass-like points. They were made in large numbers, and have the perfectly flat backs typical of machine-packed moulds.

The Shire Horse Centenary 1978 On the event of the society's centenary in 1978 Quartilles International of Coggeshall, Essex, produced a commemorative issue of horse brasses and composite face

59. The Tutankhamun patterns of 1922.

pieces inscribed 'SHIRE HORSE SOCIETY CENTENARY YEAR 1878–1978'. On the brass this appears in raised letters within a horseshoe, while on the face piece it is arranged on a flat band encircling the letters 'SHS', both the band and the initials being pinned back on to a black leather mount.

COMMEMORATIVE: PEOPLE

Fred Archer (1857–86) The supreme jockey of the 19th century, Fred Archer, nicknamed 'The Tinman', rode mainly for Lords Falmouth and Hastings. In spite of his great success, his personal life was extremely unhappy, culminating in 1886 when he shot himself. His portrait bust is usually framed within a broad horseshoe border, the hanger being supplied with an additional horizontal bar just above the top of the shoe. He is also found in a second version, bordered by a circular wreath of laurels.

Joseph Chamberlain (1836–1914) This brass, measuring some $4\frac{1}{2}$ × $3\frac{1}{4}$ inches shows the bust of Joseph Chamberlain within an oval wreath-shaped border inscribed 'ONE GREAT AFRICAN NATION UNDER / THE BRITISH FLAG'. It was made to the order of a South African farmer to commemorate Chamberlain's visit to his country in 1902–3. Very few

79

60. (*Left*) The Shire Horse Centenary, 1978.   61. (*Right*) Mr Disraeli in his
wreath of primroses, 'B.P.', Winston Churchill and Fred Archer.

of these brasses were made, but one example found in a North Devon
curiosity shop was presented to the Birmingham City Museums in 1939.

Lord Randolph Churchill Probably dating from the 1880s when
Lord Randolph was at the height of his popularity, this round brass
shows his portrait facing three-quarters to the left, against an ornamentally pierced background. The inscription reads 'LORD / RANDOLPH
CHURCHILL'.

Winston Churchill (1874–1965) In the spring of 1944, H. S. Richards
designed the 'Churchill' brass, featuring the Prime Minister's bust in
profile, complete with cigar, and supported by the victory 'V' within a
circular scallop-edged border. Having sent a specimen to Mr Churchill
for his approval, he received a reply from No. 10 Downing Street con-
veying the Premier's thanks; and giving permission for this design to
be issued after the war was over. The brass went into immediate production, however, one example being sent to President Roosevelt in
April 1944, the remainder being advertised for sale at 3s. 9d. (19p) each.

Mr Richards sent out a number of these brasses as Christmas presents
in 1944, each one having a calendar hung from it by strips of red, white
and blue ribbon.

Benjamin Disraeli, Lord Beaconsfield (1804–81) At least two horse-brass designs show the bust of Disraeli. In the first he is shown in a three-quarters view from the chest up within a circular border of prim- roses, while in the second his head alone is seen in profile, the primrose border being surrounded by a broad pierced and deeply notched band. It is likely that these brasses were produced posthumously, the Primrose League being founded in 1883 to promote the maintenance of religion, monarchy and the constitution, to improve the condition of the people and the unity of the Empire and later applying these aims to the Commonwealth.

Mr Gladstone (1809–98) The bust of Mr Gladstone is usually seen in a three-quarters view looking to the right, and details his frock coat, high collar, and broad, high forehead. It is set within an uninscribed round border edged with sixteen fleurs-de-lis.

Abraham Lincoln (1809–65) This brass was designed by H. S. Richards, who presented a specimen to President Roosevelt in April 1944. They were then offered for sale at 5s. (25p) each.

Lord Nelson Horatio, Viscount Nelson, was shot on the deck of H.M.S. *Victory* by a French sniper at the height of the Battle of Trafalgar in 1805. The brass of this popular hero, which shows his bust resplendent with sash and decorations, is surrounded by a scallop-edged border inscribed '1805'. This is not the date of the brass, however, for it appears to have been produced on the celebration of the Trafalgar centenary in 1905.

Lord Baden-Powell (1857–1941) This brass shows a portrait bust of Baden-Powell in uniform, complete with the wide-brimmed felt hat later adopted by the Boy Scouts. The round scallop-edged border is inscribed 'BADEN-POWELL / MAFEKING', commemorating his heroic de- fence of that town in the Boer War. On the reverse, the registered design number, 357452, indicates that it was introduced in 1900.

COMMEMORATIVE: ROYALTY

Brasses commemorating royal occasions form one of the largest and most popular single groups for the collector, recording every major event from Queen Victoria's Golden Jubilee in 1887 to the Silver Jubilee of Elizabeth II 90 years later. As each brass bears a relevant portrait, initials or motto, they may be readily dated. Great care should be taken to ensure that the brasses are genuinely old, however, for many have been reproduced in large numbers on subsequent occasions. Even now, brasses showing Queen Victoria and inscribed 'THE VICTORIAN RECORD 1837 – 1896' or '1837 – JUBILEE – 1887' are being cast for the tourist trade. It should be noted that brasses pierced with the initials 'G R 1727' and possibly those pierced 'V R 1870' or 'V R 1880' are relatively

62. (*Above*) Brasses commemorating the Golden Jubilee of 1887. 63. (*Below, left*) The Coronation of Edward VII, 1902. 64. (*Below, right*) The Coronation of George V, 1911. 65. (*Opposite, top*) The Silver Jubilee, 1977.
66. (*Opposite, bottom left*) The Accession and Abdication of 1936 and the Coronation of George VI, 1937. 67. (*Opposite, bottom right*) The Coronation, 1953.

modern in date. The following celebrations have all been commemorated on brasses:

1887	Queen Victoria's Golden Jubilee
1897	Diamond Jubilee
1901	Death of Queen Victoria
1902	Coronation of Edward VII and Queen Alexandra
1911	Coronation of George V and Queen Mary
1936	Accession of Edward VIII
1936	Abdication of Edward VIII
1937	Coronation of George VI and Queen Elizabeth
1953	Coronation of Queen Elizabeth II
1977	Silver Jubilee

The 'Great Seal' Various opinions have been expressed as to the subject matter of this brass; was it the fine lady at Banbury Cross, Elizabeth I, Lady Godiva, or even St Martin sharing his mantle with the beggar? 'Historian of Rickmansworth' solved the problem in 1937, quoting A. B. Wyon's *Great Seals of England* of 1887, which described the great seal of Queen Victoria as follows:

The Queen on horseback pacing to the left in a state robe wearing on her head a royal crown (without the cross arches) holding in her right hand a sceptre. . . . The horse is richly caparisoned and has a plume of three feathers on his head. The saddle cloth is closely tassellated towards the ground. A net is thrown over the hind quarters of the horse. . . . A page . . . leading the horse with his left hand.

Presumably this was made for either the 1887 or the 1897 Jubilee, an example already being in the Carter collection by 1916.

CROWNS

The crown appears on a number of horse brasses, being used on its own as opposed to being included in a specific commemorative design. At least two stamped designs are known, one showing the crown between two stars (e.g., fig. 508 in Overton's 1903 catalogue), but it is usually found in cast versions within pierced round, U-shaped, scallop-edged, laurel-wreath, or sixteen-lobed fleurs-de-lis borders.

PRINCE OF WALES'S FEATHERS

The three ostrich-feather plumes of the Prince of Wales, encircled with a coronet, form a simple yet graceful device. They appear cast in outline on a circular brass with a pierced scallop-edged border, also being modelled in relief within sixteen-lobed fleurs-de-lis design and plain, round designs, or even at the centre of an elaborate shield-shaped border. One fine heart-shaped design with the border inscribed 'EDWARD PRINCE OF WALES' was illustrated in 1916.

84

68. Royalty brasses, featuring the Great Seal, the Prince of Wales's feathers and a range of crowns.

FARMING SUBJECTS

The carters were naturally attracted to farming subjects which illustrated themselves, their tools and equipment, all the following designs being well-established by the late 19th and early 20th centuries.

The Carter Although sometimes mistaken for a shepherd, the carter stands within a variety of pierced round borders, and is dressed in a short smock and round hat, a whip being held in his right hand.

Two further designs show a cart being drawn to the left by a single horse, one version, the 'Good Carter', having the carter diligently driving his animal, while the 'Lazy Carter' is seen fast asleep in the back of the cart.

69. Farming subjects: the plough, 'Speed the plough', the carter and the 'Good Carter' driving his horse.

The Gate One version of this brass shows a freestanding four-barred gate with a diagonal brace, a hanger being attached to the top rail, a second version enclosing the gate in a circular scallop-edged border.

The Plough Ploughs are shown in at least two designs, one depicting a high-gallows plough within a round border with eight lobes around its internal edge, while the other has a plough drawn by a pair of horses, complete with ploughman within a plain round border. Occasionally, the inscription 'SPEED THE PLOUGH' appears around the border of the latter. Both these designs were known before 1916.

The Sack These brasses show a single squat sack within a round border edged with alternate ogees and pairs of semicircles, also being pierced with two horseshoe and four heart shapes.

The Sheaf The sheaf or 'garb' was a well known heraldic device, as seen on the arms of the Earls of Chester, but its appearance in a dozen or more designs is probably due to its agricultural significance. One

70. 'Hand' brasses on Ind Coope harness.

version shows three ears of wheat issuing from a fan-shaped spread of stalks, all within a plain round border, while another has the sheaf framed between a crossed pitchfork and scythe.

FIGURE SUBJECTS

The following designs, depicting a variety of subjects, were probably introduced in the years between the First and Second World Wars.

87

The Golfer This brass shows a golfer within a round scallop-edged border inscribed 'GOLF' at the base.

Shooting Here a sportsman dressed in deerstalker, jacket, and knee breeches, stands before a fence, with his dog at his side and his shotgun raised ready to fire. The round border has a ten-lobed internal edge.

The Huntsman Two or three designs show a mounted huntsman jumping over a gate, usually with the words 'TALLY HO' either at the top or bottom of the brass. Those also inscribed 'TRADE MARK' are reputed to have been used by a West Country brewery.

The Pugilist The boxer stands against a fence in the open air, his clenched fists extended to the right, all within a round scallop-edged border.

Punch and Judy These brasses, together with one of the dog Toby, have rounded borders, their outer edges being notched almost like a coarse gear-wheel. The portrait bust of Punch shows his pointed hump, his ruff and pointed hat, while that of Judy shows her holding a diminutive figure of Punch up to her enormous hooked nose.

The Rifleman This brass shows a soldier in a cross-belted tunic, his rifle being supported at his side by his crooked right arm. The border is of an elongated ogee shape with two scrolls extending to the sides just below the hanger.

NAUTICAL

The Anchor In his well-known *Heraldry* of 1610, the author Gwillim states:

The Anchor signifieth succour in extremities, and resembleth Hope . . . Because Hope doth establish and confirme our Faith against all the tempestuous Gusts of adverse occurrents.

It is found in a number of designs, both freestanding and within round borders, usually having its flukes fouled by a rope curving down from the ring.

The Dolphin Gwillim also informs us about this appealing creature:

The Dolphin is a Fish of so great a strength and swiftnesse, that when the Fishes . . . fly to the Rocks or Shoare for shelter, in the fiercenesse of his pursuit, he sometimes dasheth himself dead against the Rocke. . . . They are reported also to be great Lovers of Musicke.

The Dolphin is usually found within a pierced and scalloped eight-lobed border, or in a round border with eight lobes around its inner edge.

Fishes R. A. Brown records a circular brass edged with crescents and decorated with two fishes swimming one above the other to the left.

71. Nautical subjects: the fouled anchor, ships and a dolphin.

The Seahorse The head of a seahorse emerging from the waves is framed within a broad, flat horseshoe in this design (Richards, *All About Horse Brasses*, fig. 125).

Shells The scallop-shell design has no border, the natural form of the shell being retained except for the addition of a hanger. Most examples are stamped from thin sheet, cast scallop shells being comparatively rare.

Sailing Ships These designs all show a three-masted ship in full sail within a variety of circular borders.

Steamships In fig. 264 in *All About Horse Brasses* H. S. Richards illustrates a paddle steamer with a tall smoking funnel within a round border. He suggests that it represents the Great Western Steamship Company.

Objects

Barrels Obviously representing the brewery, barrels provided a popular device for the brasses worn by dray horses. Most examples show the barrel freestanding, either vertically or horizontally, while others have a barrel mounted on an octagonal plate, or within round borders with pierced and scalloped edges.

Bells Although a variety of brasses were designed to hold a number of miniature open-mouthed bells, the use of the bell as an ornamental design is relatively uncommon. Where it is used, however, it takes the form of a freestanding bell with a rectangular hanger.

Bicycles These are amongst the most unusual horse-brass designs, apparently having little in common with the horse. One version illustrated by H. S. Richards (fig. 304 in *All About Horse Brasses*) has a hobby-horse within a plain round border. He informs us that the original is (or was) in a Munich museum, suggesting that this might be one of the

72. Barrel and brewery brasses.

designs he produced when acting as a director of the Period Brass Company. A further version shows a tricycle of the 1880s, the seat being placed between the two large rear wheels, with stirrup-shaped steering handles and double-cranked pedals, all incised in outline on a flat round brass.

Clocks The round face of the clock made it an ideal subject for horse brasses, a number of variations of this basic theme being known.

Crescents The crescent is almost certainly one of the oldest horse-brass designs, being mentioned in Judges 8:21, when these 'ornaments like the moon' were removed from the necks of camels by Gideon. Crescents are also seen hanging from the breastband of a horse on a Roman monument now in the Römisch-Germanisches Museum in Cologne. The early collectors attributed great protective symbolism to this device, and it is possible that it was introduced into this country from Southern Europe where it was in common use, being hung points upwards, frequently enclosing a small round boss or star. They are also grouped together in threes to produce an extremely attractive brass.

The Hammer Brasses showing either a hammer or a hand holding a hammer are probably variations on the popular pub sign, the Blacksmith's Arms.

Hands Clasped hands are quite an unusual motif, but their source is well known, being a prominent emblem of Friendly Societies such as the Oddfellows, where they indicated mutual trust and friendship. The design showing a single raised hand, palm foremost, is probably based on the Red Hand of Ulster. It is found within a round border with an eight-lobed internal edge.

The Harp According to Gwillim the harp 'used in old time to signifie a man of staied and of a well composed and tempered judgement, because therein are conjoined divers distinct sounds in note or accent of accord'. However, its use on horse brasses was most probably drawn from its role as a symbol of Wales, as seen on the royal arms.

Hearts The use of the heart as a symbol of love, of death, or purely as decoration, was well known in England from the close of the medieval period. Even in outline it is a simple but beautiful shape; it appears in a great variety of horse-brass designs, often being ornately pierced and bordered.

The motif of the Heart-in-Hand is a particularly rare form, being one of the devices used by the Oddfellows Friendly Society.

The Horseshoe The combination of three horseshoes in a single brass is probably derived from the common inn sign of that name, or from the three horseshoes on the arms of the Farriers Company. Like the crescent which it closely resembled, the horseshoe was a lucky symbol, being nailed up over farm doors, etc., 'for good luck'. The single horseshoe

73. (*Opposite, top*) Heart brasses.   74. (*Opposite, bottom*) Horseshoe brasses.
75. (*Above*) A selection of subject brasses, including the Staffordshire Knot,
the Nine Elms, the clock and the shell.

appears in a number of designs, often being enclosed in a shield-shaped
scrolled border, but it is most frequently used as a frame for smaller
devices such as horses, horses' heads and lions.

Knots The origin of the Staffordshire Knot is unknown. It appears
in the centre of at least two brasses, one being a finely scrolled heart
shape, and the other a round brass enclosing an eight-pointed star. It
also appears below the Bear and Ragged Staff, this combination being
the badge of the town of Walsall.

The Lyre The classical Greek instrument had strings of equal length,
vertically strung and sounded by plucking, the pitch being regulated by

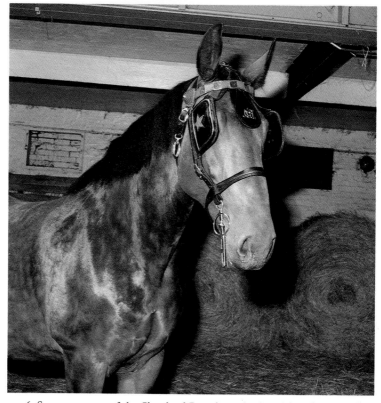

76. Superman, one of the Cleveland Bays from the Scottish and Newcastle Breweries' team, models a show bridle from the case opposite. The show harness, featuring the company's Blue Star trademark, was made at the time of the Queen's Coronation. Until then the harness had featured the initials of The Newcastle Breweries Limited.

the tension, and probably the thickness of the strings. As the symbol of music in general, it was well known throughout the 18th and 19th centuries. It is usually found in an elongated ogee-shaped scroll border.

The Microphone This is a relatively modern design, introduced between the First and Second World Wars.

The Mitre The mitre rising from a coronet occurs on the arms of the Prince-Bishops of Durham, and is found in an elongated ogee-shaped scroll border.

Playing-card Brasses The heart, the diamond, the spade and the club feature individually in numerous brasses. They also appear in groups, either being modelled simply in high relief (the heart, diamond and spade frequently being pierced to form a bold outline shape), or being

77. The display case in the Bridle Room showing some of the rosettes won by the Cleveland Bay team. The team has taken part in shows, processions and driving competitions all over the country.

seen at the centre of broad round borders pierced with concentric bands of round holes. One rare brass shows a club within a diamond within a spade within an inverted heart-shaped border.

Shields The shield shape is clearly derived from the heraldic escutcheon, and was copied from illustrations in numerous engraver's pattern books. It is found in a variety of borders on both cast and stamped brasses.

Skull and Crossbones This macabre device, together with the motto 'Death or Glory', formed the badge of the 17th Lancers, in addition to its supposed use on pirate flags. The skull-and-crossbones brass has a pierced and scalloped round border.

Square and Compasses This well known Masonic symbol often served as an inn sign. It is found in two or three different designs, one

95

78. Star brasses.

with the left caliper in front of the square, and the other with both calipers behind the square, the latter form of this symbol being incorrect.

Stars In his account of heraldic devices Gwillim tells us that the star or

Mullet in Heraldrie hath a noble signification, it being supposed to represent some divine quality bestowed from above, whereby men doe shine in Vertue, Learning, and Works of Piety, like bright Starres on the Earth.

When stars are seen on brasses, they are usually of the heraldic five- or six-pointed kind, sometimes being cast in three-dimensional form with their triangular arms rising to the central point.

Groups of stars or single multi-pointed stars are also quite common, being either cast or stamped in a variety of borders. The Star of David or Solomon's Seal, the ancient Jewish symbol of two intersecting triangles forming a six-pointed star, also appears on a number of cast brasses, either on its own, or within a border.

The Sun One of the most popular horse-brass designs, and one of the first to be widely used in this country, this device can be traced back to the sun-worshippers of antiquity. Also known as the sunflash or sunburst motif, it is found in numerous designs, often being depicted in the heraldic form of 'a sun in his glory', the round central face being surrounded by radiant beams of light. This was the sign of the Sun In-

79. Sun brasses.

surance Company; cast in lead and stamped with the policy number, it was nailed up on the insured building.

The Swastika The Swastika or gammadion was a sun symbol in prehistoric times. It enjoyed a revival as a purely decorative device early in the present century, many years before it was adopted as the official emblem of the Nazi Party and the Third Reich.

The Trefoil Trefoil designs, variously described as clubs or as the shamrock, form a popular decorative subject for both cast and stamped brasses, many of which were introduced in the Edwardian period.

The Triskelion Heraldically described as 'three Legs, Armed Proper conjoined in Fesse at the upper part of the Thigh, flexed in Triangle, garnished and spurred', the three armoured legs of the device of the Isle of Man are usually found within a plain round border.

97

80. Trefoil or shamrock designs.

PLANTS

The Acorn The oak, England's major hardwood, provided the timbers for her houses, her ships and her furniture. In addition, it was in the Boscobel Oak that Charles II safely hid after the Battle of Worcester. For these reasons the acorn was a popular symbol, being seen in a number of horse-brass designs, either alone, or surrounded by oak leaves within a variety of borders. A further design shows eight alternate acorns and oak leaves radiating from a central five-lobed leaf.

Nine Elms The Nine Elms brass shows the trees in a long row within a star-shaped opening in a pierced round border. Its origin has been variously attributed to the horses used in railway goods yard of that name near Vauxhall, London, or to those used at the Nine Elms Brewery nearby.

Fleur-de-lis This beautiful heraldic representation of an iris or lily became identified with the Royal House of France around 1139 when Louis VII of France adopted a lily on his royal ensign, Philippe Augustus making a field of golden fleurs-de-lis on a blue ground the royal arms of France. This device formed part of the royal arms of England up to the early 19th century, also being found in the armorials of various families and in the decoration of churches, where it symbolised the Trinity. On horse brasses, the fleur-de-lis may appear within a pierced quatrefoil in a tooth-edged border, but the most attractive designs are probably those in which a flat scallop-edged brass is elaborately pierced to leave the fleur-de-lis in outline against a scrolled background.

The Leek The leek, now adopted as a symbol of Wales, appears on a number of brasses of comparatively recent date.

The Rose The white rose of York and the red rose of Lancaster were united in the reign of Henry VII to form the Tudor rose, a device which has continued as a popular decorative motif through to the present day. E. V. Alison illustrates a beautiful design in which the rose is modelled in the centre of a Garter surrounded by two pierced borders, all within a plain round brass.

The 'Bonny Bunch of Roses' The rose, the thistle and the shamrock, the three undivided emblems of the British Isles, formed the 'Bonny Bunch of Roses', the symbol of a Britain unified against the threat of Napoleon.

> He took 300,000 men
> And Kings likewise to bear his train.
> He was so well provided for
> That he could sweep the world for gain
> But when he came to Moscow
> He was overpowered by the sleet and snow
> With Moscow all ablazing
> And he lost the Bonny Bunch of Roses O.

The 'Bunch' is found in a variety of borders, including a six-petalled Tudor rose design, a narrow scalloped border, a broad border pierced with eight diamonds and groups of three round holes, and a plain round border. A further design shows the 'Bunch' in outline on a flat shield-shaped brass.

The Thistle The national emblem of Scotland, the thistle proved a popular device for horse brasses, one design showing six thistle heads growing from a central six-petalled flower. This was exceptional, however, most brasses showing the head between a pair of symmetrical leaves to form a round design which could be enclosed in a variety of borders.

RAILWAY BRASSES

Up to their final withdrawal in March 1964 heavy horses had played an important part in the development of our railways, being used for many purposes. The horses were often entered in the Whit and Easter Monday shows throughout the country: Anthony Beebee Senior

81. (*Top*) The 'Bonny Bunch of Roses'. 82. (*Bottom*)
Railway-engine designs.

83. (*Above, left*) Railway monogram brasses for the Midland Railway Company, the North Eastern, and the London and North Eastern Railways.
84. (*Above, right*) The National Horse Brass Society Founder Members' Brass, 1975.

remembers drivers coming to his foundry in Walsall to have their brasses specially polished for these occasions.

Railway engines appear in a number of designs, most of them being based on locomotives of the 1860s, their boilers being sheathed in long planks of wood. Individual railway companies also issued their own monogram face pieces with elongated copperplate lettering neatly arranged within circular borders. They include 'N E R' (North Eastern Railway), 'L & N E R' (London and North Eastern Railway), 'L N W R' (London North Western Railway), 'G N R' (Great Northern Railway), and 'N S R' (North Staffordshire Railway).

Further rosettes and saddle brasses were issued by various railway companies, a comprehensive list by H. Hinchley appearing in the first edition of *Horse Brass*.

THE NATIONAL HORSE BRASS SOCIETY

Inaugurated on 22 November 1975, the N.H.B.S. has issued a unique brass to its members every year. The Founder Members' Brass, showing the Bear and Ragged Staff and Staffordshire Knot badge of Walsall, was issued to the first 107 members of the society. Each one was numbered on the reverse, a table giving the members' names appearing in the first copy of *Horse Brass*. The next brass has the initials 'H B S' on a heart within a pierced round scalloped border with the date 1976; the third has four crescents joined together as a cross with the initials spaced around the central date, 1977, while the fourth is a round scallop-edged brass pierced with an eight-petalled flower and inscribed 'N.H.B.S. 1978'. It is proposed further brasses will be issued in the coming years.

CHAPTER FIVE

Horse Bells

HORSE BELLS have a long and well documented history in England, their constant chime drawing attention both to the solitary rider and to the team as they traversed the narrow tracks and frequently unmade roads of past centuries.

Some of the earliest horse bells to be found in this country were excavated last century from London Wall, the Thames, and aptly named Little Bell Alley in the City (Borrajo, E. M. *Catalogue of the Guildhall Museums*, 1908, p. 58). Assumed to be of Roman date, they take the form of hollow spheres of iron or bronze pierced by two or four small round holes and a long rectangular slit cutting diametrically through the lower half of each bell. The bells are sounded by iron balls which are continually rolled and bounced around their interior by the action of the horse to produce a rich, sonorous rumble, quite unlike the clear notes of the open bell and clapper.

Bells of this type were certainly popular throughout the medieval period, when they served a multitude of purposes. Some were used as falconry bells, attached to the feet of the bird, others were fixed around dog collars, as seen on numerous monumental brasses; they might also be worn as personal adornment, as in the rhyme 'Ride a Cock Horse to Banbury Cross' where the lady wore 'rings on her fingers and bells on her toes'. One of the first representations of a horse bell in use occurs in the earliest illustrated book printed in the English language, Caxton's *Game and Playe of Chesse* of *c.*1476. Here the knight is mounted 'upon an hors . . . wel broken and taught and apt to bataylle and coveryd with hys armes', with the bell standing up-ended over the crupper.

By the 16th century a number of horse bells began to be made in precious metals to serve as prizes at the races. One of these 'nag-bells', some $4\frac{1}{2}$ inches in diameter and of solid silver, was presented to the Corporation of Carlisle in 1599 by Lady Dacre (Manuscript notes, Castle Museum, York). It bears the inscription:

> The sweftes horse this bel to tak
> for my lade daker sake
> H.B.M.C. 1599 [Henry Baines, Mayor of Carlisle]

At Chester Races, where bells had been offered as prizes since before

85. Caxton's knight wears a rumbler bell on his crupper, 1476.

1512, the sheriff of the city, Robert Amory, presented a magnificent set of three new bells in 1610 (Hone, W. *The Every-Day Book*, 1827, Vol. 2, p. 539). The finest was of silver double gilt and bore the arms of James I, the second, of silver, was dedicated to the princes, while the third, also of silver, was apparently undedicated. Here the bells were processed on to the course with great pomp and pageantry at each St George's Day meeting. First came:

Item   2 men in green ivies set with worke upon their other habet, with black heare and black beards, very augly to behould, and garlands upon their heads, with great clubbs in their hands, with fireworks to scatter abroad to maintain way for the rest of the showe.

It.   St. George's buckler and head-peece . . .

It.   Fame, with a trumpet in his hand . . .

It.   Mercury, to descent from above in a cloude, his winges and all other matters in pompe, and heavenly musicke with him . . .

It.   Chesters, with an oration . . .

It.   The Kyngs armes . . .

It.   The Kyngs Crown and dignity . . .

It.   1 on horseback with a bell dedicated to the Kinge, being double gilt, with

the kyng's armes upon, carried upon a septer in pompe, and before him a
noise of trumpets in pompe . . .

It.   The Prince's armes . . .

It.   An oration from the Prynce. . . .

    1 on horseback, with the bell dedicated to the princes Armes upon it, in
    pompe, and to be carried on a septer, and before the bell, a wayte of
    trumpetts . . .

It.   A cup for Saint George . . .

It.   An oracyon for Saint George . . .

It.   St. George himselfe . . .

It.   Peace, with an oration . . .

It.   Plentye, with an oration . . .

It.   Envy, whom love will comfort . . .

It.   Love, with an oration . . .

It.   The mayor and his brethren, at the Pentis of this Cittye, with their best
apparell, and in skarlet, and all the orations to be made before him, and
seene at the high crosse. . . .

Unfortunately, such spectacular celebrations were not to survive the
great upheavals of the Civil War and Commonwealth, but horse bells
continued to be made for rather more utilitarian purposes. Perhaps the
most important of these was the equipping of pack horse trains, which
carried ever increasing loads as an England still devoid of canals and
coach roads moved rapidly towards the Industrial Revolution.

Throughout the 17th and 18th centuries considerable quantities of
wool, cloth, minerals, pottery and general merchandise were readily
transported from one part of the kingdom to another by means of the
pack horse. As each animal bore its load in panniers or packs slung over
a wooden saddle, the trains were free to pass over steep hills and open
moorland by the most direct tracks, thus avoiding the circuitous vehicu-
lar routes below. In this terrain, where snow, mist and approaching dusk
could quickly reduce visibility to a few yards, it was essential to have
some means of keeping the train intact. The usual technique of doing
this is described by Thomas Bewick in his *History of Quadrupeds*, published in Newcastle in 1790, (p. 14):

In their journeys over the trackless moors, [the pack horses] strictly adhere to the
line of order and regularity custom has taught them to observe: the leading
Horse, which is always chosen for his sagacity and steadiness, being furnished
with bells, gives notice to the rest, which follow the sound, and generally without
much deviation, though sometimes at a considerable distance.

The efficiency of this system is well illustrated by memories of a team
which regularly passed through the Lake District (Rollinson, W. *Life
and Tradition in the Lake District*, 1974, p. 166):

86. Pack horse bells by Robert Wells. Calderdale Museums Service, Halifax.

. . . led by a sagacious old black stallion; their master and only attendant rode a pony and had a habit of taking his ease at . . . several inns along the route, following and overtaking the horses between his stopping places and riding on to the next, where he would rest and drink until they had plodded patiently past, when, at his own good time, he would follow and repeat the process.

Besides keeping the horses together, the sound of the bells also gave advanced warning to the traveller, the publican and the smith, that the team was about to approach, so that appropriate action might be taken.

Although relatively few sets of pack horse rumbler bells have remained intact on their original mounts, they appear to have fallen into two main classes. In the first, the bells were hung from a metal hoop rising from the front frame of the pack saddle, while in the second they were fixed at intervals along a broad leather breast band. Occasionally rumblers were also used as team bells, being mounted either in long belfries or on individual brackets rising from the hames of each horse.

Team bells were chiefly used in the south, south Midlands, and parts

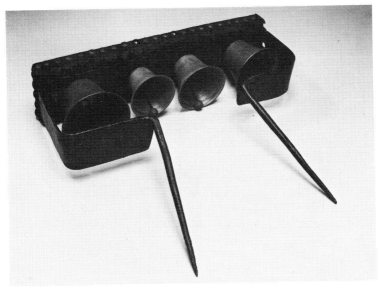

87. A belfry by Robert Wells of Aldbourne, Wiltshire.

of south Wales, the lowland areas in which four-wheeled waggons were traditionally drawn by teams of two, three, four or more horses. Here the rural lanes tended to be long, meandering and narrow, often being bounded by high banks and thick hedges. As each waggon and its team might measure some seven feet by thirty, and as there were few passing places, it was essential that the approach of a team could be clearly heard a mile or more away, so that evasive action might be taken by other vehicles.

In order to produce a sufficient volume of sound, each horse in the team was equipped with either three, four or five open-mouthed bells with swinging clappers, the combined peal often sounding the notes of two complete octaves. The bells were usually arranged in the following order, with five bells on the lead, four on the lash, and three each on the body and thill (or shaft) horses in a four-horse team. These bells were firmly fixed within long rectangular 'boxes' or 'belfries' supported above the withers of each horse by two tall iron rods which slotted into a pair of staples mounted on the hames. In the late 19th century an old west Surrey carter told Gertrude Jekyll (Jekyll, G. *Old West Surrey*, London, 1904, p. 211) how he

... always went to market with the teams dressed and the latten bells on, and when they wore *they*, the horses, were just as proud as the carters was. Each set made its own chord, while the whole clanged and jingled in pleasant harmonies.

The leather hoods covering the bells were often scalloped or evenly jagged around their lower edges, and formerly had a pretty running ornament of ears of barley incised with a small gouge into the surface of the leather. A red woollen fringe hung all around the inside of the hood, sometimes just coming a little way down, but generally being so long as to hide the bells completely. Later the fringing was abandoned and the decoration restricted to the row of close-set brass-headed nails which secured the leather back to the wooden roof of the belfry, a small heart-, oval- or diamond-shaped brass often being mounted in the middle of the front or back panels. Belfries of this type remained in use almost as long as the teams for which they were intended, still being heard in rural west Oxfordshire in the 1930s. Their clear, melodious chimes certainly enlivened the roadside scene of the 18th and 19th centuries when children would sing:

> Bell horses! Bell horses!
> What time o' day?
> One o'clock, two o'clock, three and away!

In Herefordshire and Glamorgan, the belfries took a rather different form, up to ten bells being mounted on bow-shaped iron frames

88. A pair of Shire horses cheerfully decorated for a ploughing competition.

measuring some two to three feet in width. Usually the ironwork was completely sheathed in leather to protect it from the elements, the seams being bound together with leather thongs rather than the normal stitching. Due to their great size and weight, these cumbersome belfries were fastened further down the hames than usual, an additional strap being buckled between the centre of the belfry and the saddle in order to brace the swinging load. One belfry of this type in the collection of the Welsh Folk Museum at St Fagans came from Greenmeadow, Tongwynlais, Glamorgan, and was apparently used on a local stage-coach team. Mounted on the leading horse, it warned vehicles along the route to draw to the side of the road so that the mails could get through without any delay (Peate, I. C. *Guide to . . . Welsh Bygones*, Cardiff, 1929, no. 1084).

One of the main drawbacks of the belfries was the increased weight on the horses' necks and the annoyance they caused by the constant ringing just behind the ears. For this reason bells were occasionally fixed on the waggon itself, sometimes taking the form of a leather strap bearing a number of rumblers fastened around the pole piece.

89. Mr Trimmer's waggon takes the season's hops to Alton Station,
Hampshire in 1899. Note the belfries.

In Wakefield up to 1854, the inhabitants were obliged to have all their
corn ground at the Soke Mill and so, for their convenience, a man went
around the town with a cart to collect their grain. His progress was
announced by the clanging of a large bell bound around one of the cart
shafts by a strong leather belt (original bell now in the City Museum,
Wakefield). Bells were also used on horse sleighs for a similar purpose,
the arrival of Dr John L. Kirk of Pickering being heralded in the remote
snow-covered dales of the North Yorkshire Moors by the ringing of
eight dome-shaped 'chimes', each having four clappers to obtain maxi-

108   90. A bow-shaped belfry. Hereford City Museum.

91. Dr Kirk's sleigh-bell chimes.

92. A selection of bell-brasses.

mum effect. This must have been a welcome sound to the sick or injured in the mining community of Rosedale Abbey, for here the doctor was summoned by fastening a scarf around the signpost at the foot of the dale. Local travellers recognising this signal were thus enabled to pass the call for help on to Dr Kirk as they rode on to his house in Pickering.

In addition to being used as sleighbells, these dome-shaped chimes were also mounted on the saddle where their multiple clappers would be set constantly swinging with the motion of the horse. Bells of this form were cast from the late 18th century, at least, by founders such as Robert Wells of Aldbourne, their clear sweet tones being particularly attractive.

From the middle of the 19th century most harness bells tended to adopt the traditional open-mouthed bell shape, although a number of small rumblers, either cast or stamped from thin sheet metal, continued to be made. The fly terret mounted on the head strap of the bridle provided their most popular location, cast frames holding one, two or three bells being quite common. The late Mr A. Taylor of Sevenoaks, a Past President of the Master Saddlers Federation, could remember that about 1866 his father had

... made a four-horse set of harness—one thill harness for the shaft horse, and there were three in front in rotation. The first, or leader, had three bells fixed at the top of his head, the second two bells, and the third and fourth, one bell.

His father also remembered the days of his apprenticeship at Beaconsfield, Buckinghamshire, when a firm of saddlers' ironmongers from Birmingham used to deliver their goods in broad-wheeled waggons drawn by twelve horses decorated with team bells to warn others who might meet them in the narrow roads.

Still larger frames holding perhaps seven or more bells were available to serve as decoration for the saddle or crupper strap, while further bells might be hung from purposely made rosettes or hanging horse brasses. The bright tinkling sound they emitted was certainly both gay and lively, although some waggoners developed their effect to excess, a single harness once being loaded with 320 bells!

CHAPTER SIX

Bell-founders

THE CASTING of a rumbler bell was quite a complicated process calling for a high degree of skill and expertise on the part of the mould-maker. As the final form of the bell was completely spherical, it was impossible to start making it by packing casting sand over and around a full-sized pattern, as in the case of horse brasses, for example, for it would be impossible to remove without completely destroying its impression in the sand. It was for this reason that the 'oddside' cup was introduced, this being a flanged bowl-shaped vessel just large enough to house the lower half of the bell pattern.

In use, the oddside cup was placed face-down on the moulding-board and surrounded by an inverted drag mould box. The drag was then completely filled with casting sand, rammed down, and scraped level across the top before being turned over so that the open mouth of the cup appeared uppermost.

Once the surface of the sand had been dusted with parting powder, the pattern for the bell was placed within the cup, a forked sprue piece representing the eventual hanger of the bell being plugged into two round holes situated on its top-most surface. A cope mould box was next fitted over the drag and similarly filled with sand, rammed and levelled to form the top section of the final mould.

At this stage the whole mould was turned over once more and the section holding the cup lifted off in readiness for preparing the next mould. The bottom section of the pattern revealed by the removal of the cup was then dusted with parting powder, a new drag mould being fitted around it and filled with sand to form the lower section of the final mould. Having thus completed the outer sections, they were then parted to allow both the pattern and the sprue piece to be removed, leaving a hollow hemispherical depression in both cope and drag.

If the mould were to be assembled and filled at this stage the result would be a perfectly solid ball of metal. In order to produce a hollow ball, however, a 'core' had to be made by squeezing together two hemi-spherical metal core-boxes packed full of casting sand, the round iron clapper being introduced into the centre of the core at this time. Once the core had been prepared, it was carefully lowered into the bottom half of the bell mould, where it was supported by the radial ridge of sand left to form the slot-like mouth of the bell. The cope section of the mould was then replaced over the drag and the finished mould put on one side ready for casting.

As the metal was poured from the crucible, it passed down the sprue until it had completely filled the space between the core and its enclosing walls of sand, thus forming a smooth, hollow sphere. When the mould had cooled, the bell was knocked free from the hard-packed casting sand, the core being scraped out of its mouth to leave the iron clapper permanently trapped inside. It now only remained to trim the sprue to a broad horseshoe-shaped suspension look and to clean off any casting marks, thus making the bell ready for use.

In the *Leeds Mercury* of 11 June 1728 there appeared the following advertisement:

A gang of good Pack Horses, containing eighteen in number with their accoutrements and Business, belonging to the same, being one of the ancient Gangs that has gone with Goods from York, Leeds and Wakefield to London, being the Horses of Thomas Varley; who ever hath a mind to buy them may apply to Mr William Heald at the Talbot in Wakefield, or to Lydia Varley in Lofthouse.

As this team frequently visited York, it most probably wore a set of rumblers cast by the famous Seller family, bell-founders and braziers in that city from the late 17th century through to their final closure in 1763.

It was in 1678 that Edward Seller senior was admitted to the freedom of the city as a brazier, carrying on this trade alone until joined by his eldest sons Richard, made free in 1713, and Edward, who gained his freedom in 1723 (York City Archives, Freeman's Rolls). During this period scores of church bells were cast in their foundry, together with a range of rumbler bells bearing Edward's initials 'E.S.' within the semicircular panels on each side of the basal slot.

Details of their premises are given in the elder Edward's will, proved at the Prerogative Court of York in April 1724 (Borthwick Institute, York). Here 'Edward Seller of the Parish of Saint Sampson in the City of Yorke Gentleman' bequeathed to his sons Edward and Richard

. . . all my Leasehold house or tenement with th'appurtenances situate in Jubbergate in this said City and called the Bellhouse, and likewise I give and bequeath unto my said sonns . . . equally to be divided between them all my worke tools of what kind soever belonging the Brasier trade & Bells casting.

Edward also received his father's personal estate, his house, a close of land, and a silver tankard and tumbler, while Richard was given two houses in Silver Street, a further close of land, a silver beaker and a tumbler. Following various bequests to his daughters Margaret and

Sarah, he left his third son, John, two hundred pounds, a house, and 'Five pounds more . . . upon goeing from York to London to settle there, and other Five pounds more to be paid to him as soon as he settles in London as intended'. Obviously there was to be no place for him in the family business!

Bequests of this magnitude show the elder Edward Seller to have been a man of some substance, and reflect the success of his foundry. This success was continued by his son Edward, who operated the foundry himself after Richard's death in 1724. Church bells still formed a major part of his output, these being of very high quality. On 19 May 1729, the new bells of St Martin-le-Grand, York,

. . . made by Mr Edward Seller, Bell-founder, were rung, and have been judged by most competent Gentlemen of Musick in this City, and hereabouts who approve of them to be tuneable and very fine Notes, and so pleasing, that 'tis reported that Mr Thompson will shortly present the Parish with two Bells more, to make them a peal of Eight.

These bells were finally completed on 23 December 1730, the York Society celebrating the event with a peal of Grandsire Tripples of 5,040 changes (*York Courant* entries).

The remainder of the Seller's work appears to have been involved with the manufacture and repair of household brass and copperware, as illustrated by the following notice placed in the *York Courant* of 17 November 1730:

Whereas it has been frequently reported, that Mr EDWARD SELLER Brasier and Bell-founder in this City, does not now Mend or Repair old Goods of Brass or Copper. This therefore is to advise that the Report is false and groundless; as also, that whoever shall have Occasion, cannot have their Work better done, nor cheaper, than by the above named Mr EDWARD SELLER. N.B. 'Tis also reported, that he sells Nothing by Retail, but those that have Occasion shall by Nobody be better used, both as to the Goodness of the Goods, and moderation of the Price, than by the said Mr EDWARD SELLER.

In 1733 Edward's son, John, obtained his freedom of the city, working alongside his father in the foundry. Perhaps this gave Edward the opportunity to enter into public life, as befitted his position as one of York's leading craftsmen. Throughout the 1730s and 1740s he served on a number of city committees, although he was constantly defeated in the aldermanic elections. His occasional gifts to the poor, or acceptance of pauper children as apprentices, show him to have been a responsible citizen, but he once came before the authorities charged with unloading his own coal at the staithe, instead of employing the porters. In his defence he stated that 'he was sorry for what he had done, and the same

93. (*Left*) Rumbler bell by Edward Seller of York; made between 1678 and *c.* 1760. 94. (*Right*) A rumbler bearing the initials of Robert Wells of Aldbourne, Wiltshire.

was out of ignorance of the custom and By Laws, and promised that for the future he would not offend again. . . .' His apology was readily accepted, even though we must suspect that his plea of 'ignorance' was a total invention, he being a York man born and bred.

During the late 1750s Edward retired from his various committees. He was growing old, and eventually decided to cease trading. Accordingly, the following advertisement appeared in the *York Courant* of 25 August 1761:

To be SOLD, several Houses situated in Silver Street, Jubbergate, and Newgate Street. . . . Likewise to be sold, at the lowest Prices the Household Goods, Shop Goods, Stock in Trade in the Braziery, Coppersmith and Founders Business. For further particulars inquire of . . . Mr Edward Seller, the Owner; who, on Account of his great Age, proposes declining Business. . . .

This sale was followed by a further announcement on 5 July 1763:

To be SOLD, at the Warehouse of Mr Edward Seller, in High Jubbergate, York, (by virtue of an Order from His Majesty's Court of Common Pleas at Westminster) THE remainder of the Stock in Trade of the said Mr Edward Seller, consisting of a large assortment of Braziers, Brass and Bell-Founder's Goods, together with a large quantity of Bell Metal, yellow Metal, Pot Brass, Copper Shruff &c. The Sale to begin on Thursday next, and to continue till all was sold. A large Horse Mill and Wheel, very useful for several Branches of Business will be disposed of at the above place.

It is interesting to surmise what items made up the 'Bell-Founder's Goods'. Presumably they included the moulds used for casting horse

95. An Ind Coope team of Shire horses making a delivery at The Antelope, Belgravia, London.

bells, a useful acquisition for any founder who wished to continue the Sellers' virtual monopoly of their production. Certainly they would be of no further use to Edward, for as the *York Courant* reported on 27 November 1764: 'Last Tuesday died Mr Edward Seller, formally an eminent Bell-Founder and Brazier of this City, who ser'vd the Office of Sheriff in the year 1731.'

It was in 1694 that Robert Cor first opened the foundry at Aldbourne in Wiltshire. Throughout the succeeding decades he and his family were responsible for the production of numerous church bells, ranging from their first bell of 1694 at Berwick Basset, to their last made for Great Bedwyn in 1741. In that year the foundry was taken over by John Stores who only cast some sixteen bells there before being succeeded by Edward Read in 1744. He cast even fewer church bells, but the fortunes of the foundry took a great turn for the better in 1760, when it came into the possession of Robert Wells (Julian, J. L. 'Robert Wells of Aldbourne', *The Field*, 1 August 1947).

Over the following twenty years he made between 70 and 80 bells for south country parishes, but it is not for these that he is chiefly remembered. Unlike his predecessors, he began to direct his attention to horse bells, including team bells, chimes and a series of rumblers bearing his initials 'R.W.' and size numbers from 1 to 30, the largest being 5¼ inches in diameter. The method of casting rumblers, and particularly the technique of mould- and core-making, are quite sophisticated. It is remotely possible that Wells developed the required skills through his own experiments, but considering that his bells are absolutely identical to those of Edward Seller (with the exception of the initials) it appears likely that he had access to the York founder's moulds. As these were presumably sold off between 1761 and 1763, just as Wells was commencing his business, this would have been quite possible. Wells was certainly well established as a founder of horse bells by 1772, however, for in that year he placed the following advertisement in the *Marlborough Journal*:

At the Bell Foundry at Aldbourne, Wilts, Church Bells are cast in a most elegant and as musical a manner as in any part of the Kingdom, the Founder having made the Theory of Sound as well as the nature of Metal his Chief Study; Also hangs the same, finding all materials in a complete and concise manner. And also Hand-Bells prepared strictly in Tune in any Key, *Horse bells*, Clock and Room Bells, the neatest of their several kinds, likewise Mill Brasses cast and sold at the lowest prices. All orders will be punctually observed by ROB. WELLS, Foundry. He gives Ready Money and the best Prices for Bell Metal.

In 1780 Robert Wells was succeeded by his son, also christened Robert, who operated the foundry up to his retirement in 1799. The younger Robert's brother James was made a partner in 1792, and continued to cast bells of all kinds at Aldbourne until 1826, when he sold out to Thomas Mears of the Whitechapel Church Bell Foundry in London. Most of the working stock and a number of skilled workmen were transferred to the new owners' major foundry at this time, the rumbler moulds still being in the possession of Messrs Mears and Stainbank of Whitechapel to this day. They all bear the 'R W' initials of the original Robert, as used throughout the Wells's ownership of the Aldbourne foundry from *c.* 1760 to 1826.

Further north, the Lancashire town of Wigan lay on the major north–south route now represented by the busy M.6 motorway. Bell-founding wàs already well established in this town early in the 18th century, when Ralph Ashton (active 1703–20) and Luke Ashton (1724–50) were known for their church bells and mortars. Although the numerous pack-trains passing through Wigan should have provided a ready market for the sale of rumbler bells, there appears to be little documentary evidence for their production here on a large scale. However, a number of bells cast with the inscriptions 'J.L. / WIGAN' and 'G.T. / WIGAN' have been recorded. The Wigan corporation Freeman's Rolls include a number of residents having the initials 'J.L.' but the only one of these to be described as a founder is John Latham who was elected as a burgess on 15 October 1759 and was mayor for the year 1778–9. His name is in-

96. (*Left*) A rumbler cast by John Latham of Wigan, *c.* 1760–80.
97. (*Right*) A rumbler cast by Gerald Tarleton of Wigan.

cluded in the burgess roll of 1781, but he had died by 1783. A further John Latham, burgess, is listed between 1739 and 1746, he perhaps being the father of the founder. John Latham's bells are almost identical to those of Edward Seller and Robert Wells, the inscription being contained within the double-bordered 'daisy' pattern encompassing the lower hemisphere.

In contrast, 'G.T.'s' bells have their inscriptions cast across their bases without any further decoration. A search through the Wigan archives between 1730 and 1800 has shown that the only person to whom the initials 'G.T.' are likely to refer is Gerald Tarleton (Wigan District Archives Office, Freeman's Rolls). This brazier was listed as a burgess in the town from 1738 to his death in 1753, thus giving a comparatively restricted time-scale for his products.

Today, most of the extant rumbler bells bear the 'R.W.' mark of Robert Wells and his successors, Edward Seller's bells being quite rare, while only a few examples from the Wigan foundries are known to exist. Other extremely rare rumbler bells have the initials 'W.S.', 'E.W.' or 'W.G.', but unfortunately it has proved impossible to trace any evidence regarding either their dates or their makers.

Care of Horse Brasses

THE CARE of horse brasses should present few problems to the collector, for their basic material is relatively hard wearing. For polishing, an impregnated wadding is recommended, thus avoiding the abrasive particles which might occur in pastes and creams. The brass should then be washed in warm water (a soft brush being used to clear the polish from the finer details), dried, and finally rubbed up with a warm soft cloth. The shine thus obtained will look well for perhaps a week or two but then a thin film of oxide will begin to dull the surface.

Most collectors maintain the shine on their brasses by regular polishing. Although this does show them off to the greatest advantage, it can be harmful if continued over a period of years, for every rub of the cloth slowly but surely erodes the original surface. Fine hand-finished and engraved brasses are both rare and expensive, and the collector must decide for himself whether he wishes to enjoy them in a constant highly polished form, or whether he will help to preserve them for future generations by coating them with a protective lacquer. To illustrate the problem, examples might be taken from the collection of the Castle Museum, York. There the brass bonnet of a 1909 Colibri car was carefully polished at least once a week for a period of just over ten years. As a result, the original lettering has been virtually obliterated, although it was previously quite clear. In contrast, Dr Kirk's collection of brasses, lacquered before 1935, is still in pristine condition.

When lacquering brasses, they should first be polished as instructed above, and fully de-greased with the aid of a little acetone and cotton wool swabs, great care being taken not to handle them with the fingers at this stage. Having made sure that the atmosphere is warm, dry and dust-free, a lacquer such as Incralac should then be applied with a clean brush, the brass then being left until fully dry. The slight mellowing of the shine thus produced is a small price to pay for the prolonged life of the brass.

Collections on View

A NUMBER of museums in this country hold extensive collections of horse brasses. Most of them have been given by private collectors who wished to enable the public to enjoy the products of their industry long after their deaths.

Unfortunately, due to years of under-development in staff and resources, these collections are not as readily available as their donors would have wished, many having been in store for decades. When visiting any of the museums listed below it is advisable to phone or write at least a week beforehand to discover if the collection is on view, or if the staff will be required to bring the brasses out of store for your inspection.

Beamish The North of England Open Air Museum at Beamish, near Stanley, in County Durham, includes a Home Farm, where agricultural equipment from all the northern counties is displayed in a series of restored farm buildings. One gallery is devoted to farm horses and their work in the North East, and features work harness mounted on full-size models of the local Clydesdales. The museum also houses a fine set of North Northumberland show harness, complete with fine wool decorations, made by Robinson of Millfield.

Birmingham The Birmingham City Museum Department of Archaeology houses a collection of over 300 brasses, most of these being donated by local collectors such as E. G. Harcourt and H. S. Richards, the well-known author of *All About Horse Brasses* and other books, and a director of the Period Brass Company. In addition to an excellent range of subject and pattern brasses, this collection also includes a fine series of local authority brasses for Birmingham and the surrounding boroughs.

Cardiff The Welsh Folk Museum at St Fagans Castle has a small collection of horse brasses, 31 19th-century examples having been purchased from the Lovett collection, together with a number of breast plates. The museum also possesses a pair of rumblers by 'E.W.' mounted within a leather-mounted belfry for use as team bells. There is also a set of six rumbler bells mounted on a bow-shaped iron belfry similar to those at Hereford. This example was apparently used on a stage coach near Greenmeadows, Tongwynlais, Glamorgan.

Edinburgh The National Museum of Antiquities in Edinburgh has a small collection of harness decorations, including a set of brass-mounted plough harness by T. Prentice of Carlisle, a number of decorated rein hangers, a 'Victoria / No. 22' harness bell from Alford, Aberdeenshire, and two wool and wire crowns from Fife. There are also fly terrets and bell terrets from W. B. Coutts of Newton, Alford, and 'birlers' or rotating terrets showing crown and thistle or horse head in shoe and cross designs with red plumes or 'segs' from Insch, Aberdeenshire.

Halifax The West Yorkshire Folk Museum at Shibden Hall, Halifax, has a collection of some 50 brasses attractively displayed in the old harness room, a number of these coming from a carter who lived at nearby Queensbury. In addition to the usual range of discs, hearts, diamonds, trefoils and stars, etc., there is a single R.S.P.C.A. merit badge of 1925 and a brass engraved 'BOB' from Ramsden's Brewery. A reconstruction of Winterbottom's saddler's shop houses a display of terrets, etc. and a mounted selection of makers' brasses representing saddlers in the Halifax and Huddersfield area.

Hampshire The folk-life collections of the Hampshire County Museum Service are substantially those of the Curtis Museum at Alton. Here the Curtis family built up a remarkably rich collection of agricultural material gathered from the local downland farms. The brasses include numerous face pieces, terrets and rosettes, in addition to a variety of breast plates.

There is also a good selection of bells, including rumblers by Robert Wells and Edward Seller, the latter having been worn by a ram at Odiham! There are also two four-horse sets of team bells, one coming from Lower Froyle, Alton, where they were last used in 1902, and the other from the Wykham's estate at Binsted Wyck.

Hereford The Hereford City Museum holds a small collection of brasses, in addition to sets of team bells. These are of the rare local form, six, eight, and ten bells being mounted on enormous bow-shaped iron frames, the broad ends slotting into purpose-made hames.

Hull Throughout the opening decades of the present century, the Hull City Museums were fortunate in having one of the most eclectic curators, Tom Sheppard, of whom it was said:

> Tom Sheppard, Curator,
> could beg the Equator,
> But took the firm attitude
> it was out of his latitude!

In 1938 he was able to purchase the H. Robinson Carter collection of some 650 brasses; Mr Carter was one of the earliest serious collectors, his illustrated articles published in *The Connoisseur* ('English Horse Amulets', Vol. LXV, 1916, and 'The Age of Horse Brasses', 1931) still being standard references. A selection from the collection is now displayed in the Transport Museum, Hull, and includes four panels showing the earliest designs, followed by commemorative, alphabetical agricultural, brewery and co-operative societies sections, together with a wide variety of terrets, etc.

Leicester The earliest 'horse brasses' in the Leicester Museums are those discovered in the late Bronze Age Welby hoard. Of more recent examples, however, there are about 30, most of which were acquired in two lots, one being purchased, the other being given in 1937.

London The Museum of London combines the collections of the former London Museum and the Guildhall Museum, now holding a total of well over 200 brasses. Besides the usual range of cast designs, which form the bulk of the collection, there are further examples relating to the City of London, royal events (including Queen Victoria's Golden Jubilee, and the coronations of Edward VII and George V), breweries, railway companies, the London and General Omnibus Company, and others of various unidentified firms. There are also good collections of associated brass harness furniture, dating from the medieval period onwards, including bells, buckles, rein runners, and so on.

Maidstone The Maidstone Museum houses a collection of 95 brasses, 36 of these coming from a lady in Sittingbourne, Kent. Their hangers are all well worn, and they all appear to have been well used, probably on local farms. There are a further 59 in the Carriage Museum, but their history has not yet been traced.

The museum also possesses four sets of team bells in their housings, one dated 1790 probably being the earliest yet recorded.

Oxford The Pitt-Rivers Museum, Oxford, holds the collection made by Miss Lind Eckenstein, some 165 brasses, illustrated in her article on horse brasses in the *Reliquary and Illustrated Archaeologist* of 1906. There is also a small group of St Blaise's brass horse combs from the Tyrol.

The medieval section of the Ashmolean Museum in the same town has a fine series of medieval horse decorations from Oxfordshire and the eastern counties.

Reading The Museum of English Rural Life at Whiteknights Park, University of Reading, holds some 174 brasses, including a good representative collection of cast crescents, hearts, horses, flowers, and heraldic animals, in addition to pattern brasses, etc. There are also about a dozen pressed brasses, one being an interesting copper crescent which has been polished on both sides. Most of the brasses were collected by Miss Betty Simpson, who purchased them from farm sales, etc. in Sussex in the 1920s. Other groups came here from Tunbridge Wells, and from Surrey, a further thirteen being donated by the British Council, who obtained them from a variety of sources.

Taunton The Somerset County Museum at Taunton Castle probably holds the largest public collection of horse brasses in this country, with about 1,000 specimens. Most of these are the property of the Somerset Archaeological and Natural History Society, and came to them by way of gift or bequest. The principal donors were S. Lloyd Harvey, who made several gifts in the 1920s, John Taylor, who gave 610 brasses in 1939, and John Edward Pouport, who gave 153 in 1948.

Tunbridge Wells The museum in the Town Hall, Tunbridge Wells, houses a small number of horse brasses, including a crescent, a heart, a carter and a pattern brass, all collected from Frant in East Sussex before 1937.

The sets of team bells here are of considerable interest, one set being salvaged in 1941 from a local wartime scrap dump, presumably having been used in Kent. A further set was worn by the horses of Mr George Sales, Steward of the Manor of Rusthall, when he drove annually across the Tunbridge Wells cricket pitch in order to assert the rights of the Freeholders!

Walsall The Walsall Museum holds a small collection of its own horse brasses, but this is being extended by the developing National Horse Brass Society's collection, which is placed here on loan.

Worthing The Worthing Museum and Art Gallery has a small collection of seven horse brasses and five fly terrets. However, two of the brasses are interesting friendly society award brasses of 1902, shield-shaped, and with a portrait bust of Edward VII, they are inscribed: 'R A O B, G.L. SX, WORTHING, No. 182 LODGES HORSE PARADE, GOD SAVE THE KING, 1st PRIZE, 1902'.

York The National Railway Museum, opened in York in 1975, houses some 80 horse brasses, all being either rosettes or bridle-and-harness brasses, bearing the initials of all the major railway companies.

The York Castle Museum was opened in 1938 to house the vast folk-life collections of Dr John L. Kirk, a general practitioner who had worked for the past 40 years in Pickering on the edge of the North Yorkshire Moors. His collection of some 600 brasses and bells is fully displayed here, in the former prison chapel, together with an interesting series of agricultural implements. These brasses have been used to illustrate the present volume.

Registration Marks

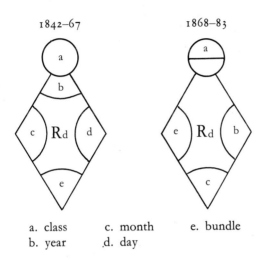

1842–67   1868–83

a. class   c. month   e. bundle
b. year   d. day

YEAR		MONTH	CLASS	
A. 1845, 1871	N. 1864	C. January	I	Metal
B. 1858	O. 1862	G. February	II	Wood
C. 1844, 1870	P. 1851, 1877	W. March	III	Glass
D. 1852, 1878	Q. 1866	H. April	IV	Ceramics
E. 1855, 1881	R. 1861	E. May	V	Wallpaper
F. 1847, 1873	S. 1859, 1875	M. June	VI	Carpets
G. 1863	T. 1867	I. July	VII	Shawls
H. 1843, 1869	U. 1848, 1874	R. August	VIII	Shawls
I. 1846, 1872	V. 1850, 1876	D. September	IX	Yarn
J. 1845, 1880	W. 1865	B. October	X	Fabrics
K. 1857, 1883	X. 1842, 1868	K. November	XI	Fabrics
L. 1856, 1882	Y. 1853, 1879	A. December	XII	Fabrics
M. 1859	Z. 1860		XIII	Lace

Registered design numbers:

1884–1910 (to 31st December each year)

1884	19753	1893	224719	1902	402112
1885	40479	1894	246774	1903	422992
1886	64519	1895	268391	1904	446387
1887	90482	1896	291240	1905	470838
1888	116747	1897	311657	1906	492874
1889	141272	1898	331706	1907	515524
1890	163766	1899	351201	1908	534097
1891	185712	1900	368153	1909	554046
1892	205239	1901	348324	1910	575180

Bibliography

Albery, W. 'Horse Brasses', *Monthly Report*, November 1940.

Alison, E. V. 'Brass Amulets', *The Connoisseur*, Vol. XXXI, 1911, p. 89.

Anonymous. 'Widespread Demand for Horse Brasses', *The Bazaar, Exchange and Mart*, 12 January 1937.

Blackmore, A. B. 'Dying Craft of the Horse Brass', *The Bazaar, Exchange and Mart*, 9 January 1934.

Bradley, G. 'Collecting Horse Brasses', *The Connoisseur*, Vol. LXXXVII, 1931, p. 81.

Brown, R. A. *The History and Origin of Horse Brasses*, Lewes 1949.

Burgess, F. W. *Chats on Old Copper and Brass*.
'A Chat on Horse Brasses', *Leather Trades Review*, 27 March 1940.

Carter, H. R. 'English Horse Amulets', *The Connoisseur*, Vol. LXV, 1916, p. 143.
'The Age of Horse Brasses', *The Connoisseur*, Vol. LXXXVII, 1931, p. 214.

Crewes, A. 'Horse Brasses: Decorative and Symbolic Harness Equipment', *Riding*, March 1940.
'More about Horse Brasses', *Leather Trades Review*, 22 May 1940, p. 434.

Drake, A. 'Horse Brasses and their Meaning', *Livestock Journal*, 16 January 1926.

Eckenstein, L. 'Horse Brasses', *The Reliquary and Illustrated Archaeologist*, New Series XII, 1906.

Evans, G. E. *The Horse in the Furrow*, London 1960.

Harcourt, E. G. 'Harness Brasses', *The Ironmonger*, 13 September 1930.

Hartfield, G. *Horse Brasses*, London 1965.

Hughes, G. B. 'Horse Brasses and other Small Items for the Collector', *Country Life*, 1964.

Jekyll, G. *Old West Surrey*, London 1904.

Julyan, J. L. 'Horse Brasses in the Motor Age', *The Field*, 20 December 1940.
'Robert Wells of Aldbourne', *The Field*, 1 August 1942.
'Armoured Horse Trappings', *The Field*, 7 April 1945.

Keegan, T. *The Heavy Horse, its Harness and Decoration*, London 1973.

McDiarmid, I. 'Horse Brasses, a Link with Long Ago', *Saddler's Journal*, 1925.

Morris, E. 'Horse Brasses in Symbol and Heraldry', *Apollo*, May 1940.

'Horse Brasses', *Monthly Report*, September 1940.

Paget-Tomlinson, E. 'Boat Horses', *Waterways News*, December 1976.

Plowright, C. B. 'Suggested Moorish Origin of Certain Amulets in use in Great Britain', *The Reliquary and Illustrated Archaeologist*, New Series XII, 1906, p. 106.

Richards, H. S. *Horse Brasses (figure subjects)*, Wylde Green 1937.

'Ancient Horse Brasses', *The Bazaar, Exchange and Mart*, 19 January 1937, p. 9.

More Horse Brasses, Wylde Green 1938.

All About Horse Brasses, Sutton Coldfield 1943.

'Horse Brasses', *Leather Trades Review*, 22 August 1945, p. 1095.

'The Victory Brass', *The Ironmonger*, 8 September 1945.

'The Victory Brass', *Riding*, Autumn 1945.

Rogers, D. 'Romance of Old Horse Amulets', *The Antique Collector*, 24 October 1931, p. 625.

Tod, A. H. *The Times*, Correspondence, 19 November 1935.

'All About Horse Brasses', *The Bazaar, Exchange and Mart*, 11 May 1937.

'Horse Brasses, Their Types and Processes', *The Bazaar, Exchange and Mart*, 18 May 1937, p. 2.

Vince, J. *Discovering Horse Brasses*, Aylesbury 1968.

Weaver, B. 'Horse Amulets', *The Country Home*, September 1908, p. 268.

ACKNOWLEDGEMENTS

In the preparation of this volume I have received great assistance from Mr Anthony Beebee Senior of Stanley Brothers, Walsall, and from Mr Terry Keegan, the well-known authority on horse brasses and founder of the National Horse Brass Society.

I am indebted to many colleagues in the museum profession, including: Miss R. Allan and Mr J. Gall of Beamish; Mr S. Price of the Birmingham City Museum; Mr C. Hendry of the National Museum of Antiquities, Edinburgh; Mr R. Innes, Mr J. Magson and Miss P. Millward of Calderdale Museum Service, Halifax; Miss A. Sandford of Hereford Museums; Mr C. Ellmers of the Museum of London; Mr R. A. Rutland of the Leicestershire Museums Service; Mr G. Hunter of Maidstone Museum; Mr R. Brigden of the Museum of English Rural Life, Reading; Mr P. Saunders of the Salisbury and South Wiltshire Museum; Mr P. Stevens of the Somerset County Museum, Taunton; Miss M. Gill of Tunbridge Wells Museum; Dr G. Bowie of the Hampshire County Museum Service, Winchester; Mr J. Norwood of Worthing Museum; and Mr J. Woods of the National Railway Museum, York. I am also most grateful to Mr Gillies of the Wigan Record Office for his help.

Special thanks are also due to Mrs Rosemary Ellis for allowing me to reprint her excellent photographs of working horses (pp. 18, 25, 41) and to the following for supplying photographs from their collections: The Ashmolean Museum, Oxford (p. 8); The Birmingham City Museum (pp. 28–32 (*top* and *above*), 79); Calderdale Museum Service, Halifax (p. 105, top); Hampshire County Museum Service (p. 108, top); Hereford City Museum (p. 108, bottom); Ind Coope Breweries (pp. 46, 87, 115); The National Horse Brass Society (p. 101, right); The Salisbury and South Wiltshire Museum (p. 14, bottom); Scottish and Newcastle Breweries (pp. 47, 94, 95); and Sally Anne Thompson (pp. 22, 23 107). The remainder of the photographs were skilfully prepared by Mr Ken Shelton of York from the Kirk Collection of brasses in the Castle Museum, York; the painting in the Frontispiece is also from that museum.

Most of all, I wish to thank Mrs Moyra Johnson for her great care in translating my manuscript into readable typescript.

Publisher's note: The drawing on p. 24 is by the author.

Index

N.B.: Page numbers in *italic* refer to illustrations where these
are separated from the text.